AND FUTURE

Ancient World Studies in Australia

edited by Robert Sinclair

Commemorative volume of *Antichthon*

Australian Society for Classical Studies

Published by
Australian Society for Classical Studies

National Library of Australia
Cataloguing-in-Publication entry:

Past, Present and Future: Ancient World Studies in Australia.

Includes bibliographies.
ISBN 0 646 01615 6.

1. History, Ancient. I. Sinclair, R. K. II. Australian Society for Classical Studies.

930

Printed by Australian Print Group, Maryborough, Victoria
Typeset by Midland Typesetters, Maryborough, Victoria
Designed by Diane Quick

CONTENTS

EDITOR'S PREFACE

The Australian Society for Classical Studies was established in 1965–6 with the object of advancing the study of ancient Greece and Rome and related fields. Its major activities have been the holding of academic conferences and the publication of the journal *Antichthon*, which publishes articles on topics relating to the languages, literature, thought, history and archaeology of the ancient world.

The Society decided to commemorate its twenty-fifth anniversary with a volume of essays. There is strong evidence of widespread interest in the ancient world—witness community support for departmental museums in the universities and for exhibitions in national and state galleries and museums, or the strength of demand for public lectures and for courses at secondary and tertiary levels. The Society therefore decided that this commemorative volume should convey to a wider audience the interests and activities of scholars working in Australia in the field of ancient world studies. While informative and illuminating, the articles were not intended to be replete with scholarly detail. Fourteen contributors have been asked to write articles reflecting some of the major areas of interest in the ancient world and exploring questions of general significance in their own right, while giving some indication of advances in the field in the past twenty-five years and possibilities and trends in the future. Some indication of the range of fields which it has not been possible to include in this volume can be gained by consulting the list of books published in the years from 1965 to 1990 by scholars working in Australia in the field of ancient world studies.

The debts of an editor are many. It is a pleasure to acknowledge the enthusiasm and hard work of a very active editorial committee—Alan James, Beryl Rawson and Greg Stanton—and the ready support of the executive committee and university representatives of the Society. The cooperation of the contributors and the efforts of Fred Van Steel at Australian Print Group, Midland Typesetters and the designer, Diane Quick, have greatly assisted our work. Permission to reproduce material is gratefully acknowledged, and in particular the willingness of the Curator of the Nicholson Museum in the University of Sydney, Alexander Cambitoglou, to agree to reproduction of the Nicholson Hermes on the cover. For many the Nicholson Hermes symbolises the significance and the continuity of ancient world studies in Australia.

September 1990 Robert Sinclair

FOREWORD

Classical studies are alive and flourishing in Australia. That is the first thing that is apparent from this collection of essays. They commemorate twenty-five years of commitment by scholars in the Australian Society for Classical Studies. In a period in which the study of Greek and Latin authors, and of the glory that was Greece and the grandeur that was Rome, has not been pressed as a matter of great moment for Australia, scholars have shown that like students they can vote with their pens if not with their feet. Australian classical scholars know that the ancient world is interesting and worth knowing about, and they suggest—at least by implication—that in Australia we neglect that world at our peril.

A second observation may be pertinent. These essays give examples of the variety of skills and disciplines necessary for understanding that ancient world: literary criticism, artistic insight, historical and archaeological investigation, philosophical analysis are all necessary if we are to understand Greece and Rome. They are also necessary if we are to understand our own culture and civilization. It is not without significance that classical scholars have frequently turned their trained minds to the elucidation of contemporary life. Long may they do so. We would not be thinking and writing and living as we now do in 20th century Australia had it not been for people who lived and events which occurred two thousand and more years ago. We should be grateful to those scholars who keep that world before us, illuminating our minds and quickening our imagination. We should wish them well.

Government House, Melbourne — J. Davis McCaughey

ILLUSTRATIONS

AUSTRALIAN CLASSICAL STUDIES AND MEDITERRANEAN ARCHAEOLOGY

Graeme Clarke
Humanities Research Centre,
Australian National University

Archaeological work on past civilizations seems always to capture immediate and popular fascination. Not only does it hold something of the simple lure of detective sleuthing but it holds out as well the perennial hope of winning new knowledge of the past, particularly knowledge that adds to our sense of immediacy of living in the past, knowledge often denied us by the information that has come down to us selectively filtered and already mediated by our ancient literary sources. Classical studies in Australia have always been strong in the study of ancient history, and much involvement in archaeological work by Australian scholars has consequently arisen *via* the urgent need to supplement and flesh out our written sources so that scholars can start to ask and attempt to answer new questions about ancient society—as well as to provide fresh insights into the social conditions and historical contexts for understanding the production of the ancient literary texts themselves.

But it must be appreciated that archaeological work can be enormously varied and by no means need involve the special skills of actually unearthing an archaeological site. In some senses what is often needed in ancient archaeology is not new information but fresh interpretative work on existing information held in museums, collections of antiquities, in published reports or to be derived from actual monuments already excavated. Work currently being carried out in the Mediterranean by Australian classical scholars involves such projects as the systematic re-examination of such major Roman architectural monuments and social institutions as Roman baths, Roman theatres and Roman amphitheatres (DeLaine, Sear, Jory, Green, Farrington), or the systematic examination and analysis of cultural assimilation and regional difference in the monuments of such major cities as Petra, in Jordan, and Alexandria, in Egypt (McKenzie). A particularly important project of this kind has been the systematic and thorough recording (architectural and decorative) of several major houses in Pompeii, excavated long ago but never fully published (Descoeudres, Sear, Green and others); fast disappearing knowledge has been rescued and important new detailed information added by such work.

Museum work on already excavated Cypriot pottery (but inadequately or never published) is adding greatly to the corpus of our knowledge of Bronze Age Cypriot society in its economic, religious and social aspects (Merrillees, Webb); and the life-time's work of Emeritus Professor Dale Trendall on South Italian pottery has been of fundamental importance for the recovery of accurate chronology and the rich cultural life of Greek settlers in Southern Italy. Museum work on already unearthed epigraphic texts is adding greatly to our detailed knowledge of the public workings of Hellenistic society, especially in Athens, aspects of society for which our literary sources often fail us, or mislead us (Osborne, Henry, to name but two out of many). And computer work is aiding greatly in the compilation of epigraphic data bases for analysing the demography provided by tombstones and similar monuments (Osborne for Attic society, Jory, Weaver and Gallivan for Imperial Roman society).

". . . whole areas of the ancient world, largely lost to us if we rely on literary sources alone, are being opened up to us . . ."

Such work, supplemented by other archaeological monuments and legal texts, can be made to enhance our understanding of institutions so fundamental to the constitution of ancient societies as slavery, the family and private life (Weaver, Rawson, Dixon and others). And whole areas of the ancient world, largely lost to us if we rely on literary sources alone, are being opened up to us by the regional study of epigraphic texts and monuments (for example, Bryce on Lycia in South West Turkey, Horsley on Pisidia in Southern Anatolia), or by the close study of hitherto unassimilated finds such as non-literary papyri from ancient Egypt (Whitehorne, Pickering and Judge). Equally important, fresh insights into our understanding of the ancient texts themselves, so important for our cultural traditions, can be gained by bringing to bear such new details of the workings of contemporary society, or the contemporary nuances of particular linguistic usages, as Horsley, Judge and others are doing for the New Testament documents.

Important archaeological work can be carried out in the field but still does not involve actual excavation. Survey work is one such. In Southern Jordan, for example, the 'Aqaba-Ma'an Archaeological and Epigraphic Survey has recovered a remarkable series of petroglyphs and inscriptions adding much to our appreciation of nomadic or transhumance Nabataean life (Jobling), whilst in Northern Turkey, inland from the Black Sea, survey work is revealing migration and settlement patterns by the technique of identifying and sherding archaeological sites (Sagona). In Eastern Turkey survey work is also adding much to our understanding of provincial Byzantine life and culture by a systematic examination of the decorative programmes and liturgical furnishings and functions of the rock-cut churches of Cappadocia (Grishin, Wallace): similar work is being done on the floor-mosaics of Byzantine churches in Palestine (Henderson).

Some work is impelled by the salvage of endangered archaeological evidence. Several Australians are involved in the Tishreen Dam Salvage in North Syria, surveying and excavating important sites threatened to be destroyed by the lake to be formed by a new dam across the Euphrates (Bunnens at Tell Ahmar, Porter and Mottram with a Chicago-Syrian team). Others are involved with maritime archaeology (e.g. Hillard on the Harbour installations at Caesarea Maritima in Israel) or sepulchral Egyptian archaeology (Kanawati at El Hawawish), thereby recovering much sense of the aspirations of provincial life.

Meantime the painstaking work of excavating particular sites on a regular basis is being carried out by a number of Australian teams. In Southern Italy a team is excavating the site of I Fani in the province of Lecce, promising to provide a significant contribution to the study of the relationship between the native Messapian population and the early immigrant Greek colonists (Descoeudres, Robinson, Gollan). In Northern Greece the very important classical site of Torone has been regularly excavated since 1975 by a large team under the direction of Cambitoglou, illuminating many aspects of Greek life from the Bronze Age onwards; and the Early Iron-Age cemetery of Kouko near Sykia in Chalcidice is being excavated by Carington Smith. At the same time, since 1979, under Hennessy's direction, the major city of Pella in Northern Transjordan (Tabaqat Fahl) has been systematically excavated in collaboration with Wooster College, Ohio, USA and has yielded important remains ranging all the way from the palaeolithic to the mediaeval periods. These excavations give important on-site experience for Australian students, broadening and deepening their perspectives and training in classical studies.

At base all these activities by Australian archaeologists and classicists are but facets of dissecting ancient societies of the Mediterranean, endeavouring to perceive how they organized themselves along with all their ethnic and regional variations, how they managed their social, economic, religious and political lives, how they expressed the way they saw themselves and their world through their artefactual and cultural achievements, how they laid out their towns and exploited and settled their lands, how they adapted to changing circumstances and conditions. These are basic questions that one needs to ask of any society, and by asking them and seeking answers to these inquiries Australian researchers are deepening our understanding and appreciation of the humanistic achievements of Mediterranean cultures of the past—and accordingly of our own. It is deep-set within classical studies that the proper study of mankind is man.

It may be helpful to describe in a little more detail the work on one classical site as a sample of this sort of activity.

". . . Australian researchers are deepening our understanding and appreciation of the humanistic achievements of Mediterranean cultures of the past—and accordingly of our own."

When an Australian team was excavating the Middle Bronze Age site of El-Qitar in the early eighties (Culican and McClellan), a site on the Euphrates in North Syria, a survey was carried out in the surrounding terrain to discern settlement patterns and land usage of later periods in the hope that this might throw light on the Hittite management of the region. In the course of this survey an archaeological site (known locally as Jebel Khalid) was discovered a few kilometres to the south of El-Qitar, and subsequent sherding and systematic survey showed that a major classical site had been found. A large limestone outcrop, some kilometre and a half in length along the west bank of the Euphrates and covering some fifty hectares of undulating land, had been walled on its inland sides along with a separate acropolis, enclosed within the outer walls, situated on the highest ground, and itself defended by walls that enclose over two hectares of land. The river bank, consisting for the most part of high cliffs, was left to a large extent unwalled. Sherding indicated at least Hellenistic occupation. Subsequent study revealed that there were nearly four kilometres of wall along with some twenty-eight interval towers: the construction of regular ashlar blocks in a standard header and stretcher arrangement and the circuit curtain-walling, clinging to the outmost perimeter of the Jebel wherever possible, strongly pointed to Hellenistic building and defensive techniques. Sample excavation has confirmed this deduction, with Hellenistic material recovered from the foundation trenches: the walls were built upon virgin soil excavated to bedrock socles. One massive semi-circular tower (18 metres by 15 metres) was chosen for intensive study. Already a sense of what it might be like to have come as Macedonian settlers in the wake of Alexander the Great's conquest had started to emerge. These beetling towers and massive walls (nearly three metres thick) would have stamped imperial authority upon the landscape visible for kilometre after kilometre: and though the Jebel is in the heartland of Seleucid territory, the human endeavour of quarrying, surveying and constructing this elaborate defence system tells its own story of insecurity in a foreign landscape, still felt to be at risk. This impression of conquering authority has received further reinforcement by the excavations of the Main Gateway. Two huge forward-projecting rectangular towers, each over sixteen metres wide, stood guard over the entrance to the town, sheathed elegantly in orthostat cladding. They would have daunted any visitor who entered under their shadow by the paved roadway of the actual gateway (found in excellent condition several metres below present ground level). The Greek colonists had come to stay and to command authority over their surrounding territory. Their drive and energy are manifest.

The town, occupying some three-fifths of the Jebel, was laid out on a Hippodamian grid with streets running strictly east-west, north-south. No evidence of pre-Greek occupation has been found. The Greeks had carefully chosen a virgin site at a river-crossing point and set up a new town which would have acted as a control point in river traffic (trade going all the way down to the Persian Gulf and continuing for at least 120 kilometres further upstream). Excavation of the domestic housing is still at an early stage but it has already revealed large, many-roomed dwellings with some pretensions (paved entrance ways from the street and impressively massive doorways). A long rectilineal building divided into a number of smaller rooms appears to have been a stoa or row of shops. It remains to be seen how these houses compare with contemporary Hellenistic dwellings in mainland Greece and whether the immigrants adapted to local conditions and materials and perhaps changed over time as they settled down more comfortably with the local population. So far the analysis of the evidence shows remarkably little permeation of local cultures into the Hellenistic material remains, but much work still remains to be done and it is premature to draw any conclusions.

Work on the public building area is yet to commence but it will tell us importantly what Greeks at the period of establishment regarded as essential amenities for urban living and whether, again, the original planning became modified as the population itself may have modified with intermarriage and acculturation. Even so, the visitor, looking up to the Acropolis, would have seen an impressive statement of Greek values. Around a cavernous courtyard cistern was erected an extensive administrative and domestic building, with a Doric-order colonnade around the four sides of the courtyard. The task was monumental, with the columns on the entrance side over a metre in diameter at their base. One large public room over fourteen metres long was entered

Measuring and drawing a drum-altar in situ *at Jebel Khalid: B. Raworth.*

Rosette, guttae and lion-headed waterspout from Doric colonnade, Acropolis, Jebel Khalid.

by a double-leaved doorway, flanked by pillars and embellished by pilasters and pilaster capitals in the room's corners. A massive tapering column set up on a high plinth of bedrock stood in the centre of the room to support the roofing of this room. The whole room was carefully plastered, including the columns, largely in white; traces of red and blue paint have been found on the cornice mouldings. And one wall of the room was decorated in Pompeian first-style masonry wall-painting, an elaborate technique consisting of a series of raised panels painted in *trompe l'oeil* marbling. Over twenty different marbling combinations have been recovered along with some floral motifs. This

"Jebel Khalid has proved to be a unique site in this part of the Middle East . . ."

complicated form of decoration was regarded by Hellenistic Greeks as the acme of civilised living, and here in a new and distant land amid an alien population they had gone to great pains to reproduce the hallmark of their home culture. These immigrant Greeks had great confidence in their Hellenic values and had determinedly stamped them on this new landscape.

Jebel Khalid has proved to be a unique site in this part of the Middle East—a purely Greek site without earlier or later occupations. An opportunity is thus provided for writing an absent chapter in the history of Hellenistic Syria—how Greeks laid out new towns along the Euphrates at strategic intervals to guard and control the river highway and what it was like to live as imperial colonists in a land already long settled by native populations with their own traditional value systems. It may be possible to detect new local tastes in formation over time. It is work not without its resonances for Australians, and students and staff from many Australian universities (Western Australia, Adelaide, Melbourne, Australian National University, Sydney) have already participated in the work on Jebel Khalid.

Jebel Khalid started out as part of survey archaeology and now it has aspects of salvage archaeology as the site is threatened by the construction of the Tishreen Dam adjacent to the Jebel. Work must continue each year to recover as much information as possible before it is irretrievably lost. Dura Europos is a more famous station further down the Euphrates but its Greek phase is almost totally lost; Jebel Khalid is its Greek clone and will now be able to supply in large part its lost history.

THE ART AND ARCHAEOLOGY OF THE ANCIENT MEDITERRANEAN WORLD

PROGRESS AND DEVELOPMENTS IN ITS TEACHING AND PRESENTATION

A.D. Trendall
La Trobe University

The art and archaeology of the ancient world (Egypt, the eastern Mediterranean, Greece and Rome) is a comparatively recent addition to the range of courses offered by Faculties of Arts or Humanities in the universities of Australia. It was introduced at Sydney in the years immediately following the Second World War and has, since then, become more widespread, with a variety of courses now available in at least ten universities. As it is a matter of crucial importance that students enrolled in such courses should have direct access to a reasonable amount of original material, the past forty years have seen not only a steady increase in the number of teaching collections in universities but also a growing Australian participation in excavations at several ancient sites in the Mediterranean area (notably in Egypt, Jordan, Syria, Turkey, Cyprus, Greece and South Italy), through which both teachers and advanced students are able to gain first-hand experience of work in the field, and which, in the case of countries which permit a limited export of excavated material, may also provide a useful source for additions to the teaching collections in this country.

Since Australia's connection with Egyptology is dealt with in some detail by Robert Merrillees in his recent work *Living with Egypt's Past in Australia*, only brief references are made to it in the present article. It is interesting to note that Monash University has just established a Centre for Egyptian Studies—the first of its kind in this country.

Until the 1950s Sydney was the only university to possess a major collection of antiquities. This was due to the foresight of Sir Charles Nicholson, its Chancellor, who in 1860 presented to it the extensive collection of Egyptian and Classical antiquities which he had acquired during his Mediterranean travels and which, with a vision well ahead of his times, he saw would be of much greater value as a teaching aid in Australia than in England. His collection included a large number of Greek vases, a few examples of Etruscan and Roman sculpture, as well as some 70 sepulchral inscriptions, including several of particular interest relating to the Roman fleet at Misenum. In 1934 the sons of Sir Charles, to commemorate the centenary of their father's arrival in Australia, presented to the University the statue generally known as the Nicholson Hermes, a Hellenistic or Roman copy of a Greek original of the type made popular by Praxiteles and his followers. It was originally the property of Sir George Macleay, who had acquired it in Turkey and who gave it to Sir Charles in 1881.

The collection was greatly expanded by Professor W.J. Woodhouse during his tenure of the chair of Greek and, after his death in 1937, through the good offices of Professor Samuel Angus, who acted for a while as Curator, and was instrumental in securing for the Museum the Deissmann collection of ostraka and the A.B. Triggs collection of coins. Professor Trendall followed as Curator in 1939, but the subsequent outbreak of war necessitated the closing of the Museum and the abandonment of a newly-instituted course in ancient art and archaeology. The Museum was able to re-open in 1946 and the abandoned course was resumed in a slightly modified form. It proved attractive to students and in 1948 a department of Archaeology was established, with Professor Trendall in the chair; J.R.B. Stewart was transferred from Ancient History to become the Senior Lecturer. He was a specialist in the archaeology of Cyprus and the Near East, the study of which now became an important element in the courses offered by the new department, and he greatly expanded the Museum's holdings in those areas with material from his own excavations or acquired on the market. The same period also saw many notable acquisitions of Greek antiquities, mostly from various private collections in England, Europe and America, dispersed after the war and sold at auction.

Soon after the departure of Professor Trendall to become Master of University House at the Australian National University in Canberra in 1954, the University received a handsome bequest to endow the Edwin Cuthbert Hall Chair of Middle Eastern Archaeology, to which J.R.B. Stewart was appointed in 1960. After his untimely death two years later, Alexander Cambitoglou was appointed to a chair of archaeology, the Edwin Cuthbert Hall endowment being allowed to lie fallow for some years, until the appointment of Basil Hennessy in 1973. Five years later in 1978, Sir Arthur George provided an endowment for the Renée and Arthur George Chair of Classical Archaeology, which was then occupied by Professor Cambitoglou, who held it until his retirement in 1989, when he was succeeded by Dr J.R. Green. Sydney is therefore particularly fortunate in having endowed chairs in both Middle Eastern and Classical Archaeology; it is as yet the only university in Australia to have specific chairs in either field. At Melbourne, the recent amalgamation of Classics with Middle Eastern Studies has created a new department of Classical and Near Eastern Studies and has brought together four staff members in the combined field, who are able to provide a full range of courses in Mediterranean art and archaeology. At other universities such courses are sometimes given in Departments of Art History or Archaeology, though the latter are normally more closely concerned with Australia, South East Asia and the Pacific.

Under the direction of Professor Cambitoglou the Nicholson Museum at Sydney has been completely reorganised; in 1966 it was opened in a new and much improved form, with the more important antiquities on display in the redesigned former premises and the remainder in a new gallery on the floor below. In its present state it can certainly hold its own with most of the comparable university museums in England and America. Recent years have also witnessed the purchase of many notable antiquities—vases, bronzes, sculpture and terracottas—which have greatly enhanced the collection and filled in some of the more obvious gaps. The Friends of the Nicholson Museum and of the Australian Institute of Archaeology in Athens, the latter established in 1981, with Cambitoglou as its first and present Director, have made notable contributions towards the purchase of antiquities.

Also in Sydney, at Macquarie University, a significant teaching collection of some 4000 antiquities has been built up since 1976, in which Egypt and the Near East are well represented, thanks to the efforts of Dr. N. Kanawati, and the loan from the Australian Museum of some material from Garstang's excavations at Beni-Hasan at the beginning of this century.

The University of New England in Armidale (NSW) also has a Museum of Antiquities, with a Classical and a Prehistory section, the latter being mainly concerned with the life and work of the Australian Aborigine. The former includes a good selection of Cypriote and Middle Eastern material, especially from Stewart's excavations at Palaealona and from his private collection, as well as representative examples of Greek pottery and a selection of ancient coins.

The Department of Classics and Ancient History at the University of Queensland set up in 1963 an Antiquities Museum, which has now reached very respectable proportions and covers a fairly wide range, thanks especially to the efforts of Bruce Gollan and support of the Alumni Association, which provided funds for the purchase of a Greek helmet and for a number of Greek vases. There is also a small collection in the Abbey Museum at Caboolture, which is particularly strong on the Cypriote side.

The Australian National University in Canberra has, since 1962, built up a good collection, now well displayed in the Department of Classics in the A.D. Hope Building. It includes the Greek vases formerly in University House, as well as the Apulian tomb-group acquired by the University in 1965, together with a number of subsequent purchases, among which is a selection of finds from the Late Bronze Age temple at Amman, a number of lamps from various periods, representative examples of small bronzes and terracottas, and of Greek and Roman glass, as well as of Greek and Roman coins.

The museum attached to the newly-formed department of Classical and Near Eastern Studies at the University of Melbourne has an extensive collection, especially of ancient coins, which had as its nucleus the representative selection of Greek vases acquired around 1930 as a memorial to John Hugh Sutton. This has been extensively supplemented in the post-war years by extensive purchases and acquisitions, especially of Cypriote material from the excavations of J.R.B. Stewart and from the collection of the Australian Institute of Archaeology in Melbourne. There is also on loan a representative selection of Greek vases from the Geddes collection, currently housed in the University Gallery. Loans from this collection have also been made to La Trobe and Monash Universities, both of which have small collections of their own, as well as to the University of Queensland.

In Hobart, at the University of Tasmania, a small museum of antiquities has been built up under the energetic and enthusiastic direction of Ronald Hood; it has been named after John Elliott, who held the chair of Classics there from 1941 to 1966 and was a keen supporter of the value of teaching collections. Its particularly attractive display well illustrates what can be achieved with a limited budget by the exercise of ingenuity and imagination. The same might be said of the Museum of Classical Archaeology, opened in 1983, in the University of Adelaide, which has since progressed with an enviable rapidity under the guidance of Dr Frank Sear.

The fact that no fewer than ten of the universities of Australia now have teaching collections of Mediterranean antiquities, only two of which go back to the pre-war period and most of which have come into being during the past thirty years, can only be regarded as a testimony to the increasing popularity of the studies for which they provide the original material, and of the perceived value of this as a stimulus not only to students working in this field but also to the wider public, whose interests in it have been aroused both by archaeological programs on TV and by the several important exhibitions which have come to Australia in recent years.

One result, as has already been mentioned, of the growing interest in Mediterranean archaeology has been a steady increase in the degree of Australian participation in excavations in that area. In 1951 an expedition sponsored by the University of Sydney, in conjunction with the Ashmolean Museum in Oxford, went to Cyprus to excavate, under the direction of Basil Hennessy, a Bronze Age cemetery at Stephania; shortly after, in 1955, Stewart excavated at Ayia Paraskevi and Vasilia, and in 1960 at Palaealona and Lapatsa, under the auspices of the University of Melbourne, with the support of various English, New Zealand and Australian institutions. Hennessy returned to the Near East in 1966 to excavate a Late Bronze Age temple near the Amman airport, and again between 1975 and 1978 at Teleilat Ghassul, at the northern end of the Dead Sea. Since 1979 he has been excavating, with spectacular success, at Pella in Jordan, in collaboration with Wooster College, Ohio, and with the support of the University of Sydney and the Australian National Gallery in Canberra. Support for these projects has also been provided by grants from the Australian Research Council (ARC), which has also assisted the Australian Expedition to Pompeii, the Macquarie University expedition to Egypt, the University of Melbourne's excavations at both the Bronze Age site of El-Qitar and the Hellenistic site of Jebel Khalid in northern Syria, in the latter of which the Humanities Research Centre of the Australian National University in Canberra has also participated. The ARC has likewise given generous financial support to the excavations in Greece conducted by Professor Alexander Cambitoglou, first at Zagora on the island of Andros between 1967 and 1977 and since 1975 at Torone in the Chalkidiki in northern Greece. The former, after ten excavation campaigns, yielded results of unique importance for our fuller understanding of Greece in the Geometric period, and the finds are now splendidly housed in the Archaeological Museum of Andros, thanks to a generous donation from Basil and Elise Goulandris. Torone, where since 1986 the excavations have also been supported by the Australian Archaeological Institute in Athens, has also brought to light material of paramount importance, especially for the Proto-Geometric period. An early Iron Age site at Koukos, near Sykia, also in the Chalkidiki, is in process of excavation under the direction of Dr Jill Carington Smith, with the support of the University of Tasmania. In South Italy an Australian team led by Frank Sear and J.-P. Descoeudres, with members drawn from several of our universities, has collaborated in the international project 'Pompeian Houses', designed to record and publish a number of houses in danger of suffering irreparable damage to the paintings on their walls or to their structure. Still more recently a team from the Universities of Sydney and Queensland has begun a systematic study of the site 'I Fani' in southern Apulia, in collaboration with Dr Francesco D'Andria of the University of Lecce, the Archaeological Superintendency of Puglia and other Italian

A 5th century BC lekane, (a wide shallow bowl) found at Torone during the 1981 excavation. Possibly made locally.

and European institutions. This should yield results of considerable importance for the history of the Salentine area after the Greek settlements there from the eighth century BC onwards.

In 1988 an expedition, initiated by Dr A. Sagona of the University of Melbourne, began a systematic survey of ancient sites in the Bayburt province of N.E. Turkey. It should be noted that Australians have also taken part in many other excavations sponsored by various institutions at a number of other ancient sites—e.g. in Egypt, where Dr Colin Hope has worked with the Canadians at the Dakhleh Oasis, and Dr Lisa Giddy at Memphis; on the Jerash International Project; at the excavations of the University of Michigan at Carthage; at the American excavations in Corinth.

With all this work in active progress it is little wonder that the time was thought to be ripe for the publication of a local journal which could keep scholars abreast of the latest discoveries in the Mediterranean area, and in 1988 appeared the first volume of *Mediterranean Archaeology* (*Meditarch*), under the editorship of J.-P. Descoeudres, an Australian and New Zealand journal for the archaeology of the

Mediterranean world, with up-to-date accounts of the latest excavations.

While it is clear that considerable progress has been made in building up collections of antiquities in our universities, it is a pity that our public museums and galleries have not yet followed suit. The only public collection of ancient art of any importance is that of the National Gallery of Victoria, which contains a good selection of Roman glass, some mummy portraits and sculptured heads, and since 1957, largely through the support of the Felton Bequest, it has been able to acquire a small but very distinguished collection of Greek pottery, including a Geometric hydria by the Analatos Painter, several outstanding examples of Attic black- and red-figure vase-painting, a white-ground lekythos by the Achilles Painter, as well as several South Italian vases of particular interest for their subject-matter. It is to be regretted that these works are temporarily in storage, since their absence from the Gallery's display prevents the public from seeing some of the finest Greek vases in this country. A few Egyptian, Greek and Roman antiquities have found their way into other galleries or museums, notably the South Australian Museum in Adelaide (of which there is a typescript catalogue by M.J. Watson, listing 37 items), the Victoria Museum in Melbourne, the Australian Museum and the Museum of Applied Arts and Sciences in Sydney, but they contain few items of particular importance. The Australian Institute of Archaeology housed in 'Ancient Times' house in Melbourne is a private foundation, established in 1946 by the late W.J. Beasley to support biblical studies; it retains a part of its original collection, mainly of Cypriote and Near Eastern antiquities; much of the rest has now passed to the University of Melbourne. The Australian National Gallery in Canberra has some valuable material from Hennessy's excavations at Pella, but its chief glory from the ancient world is the magnificent Early Cycladic 'idol' by the Goulandris Master, which, according to Dr P. Getz-Preziosi, the leading authority in this field, displays 'a calm force, a harmony of proportion, and a refinement of line which characterize the finest examples of Early Cycladic sculpture'.

As yet there are few substantial private collections of antiquities in Australia, though the number of collectors would appear to be increasing, as a significant growth in the number of dealers in this field indicates. The largest is the Geddes collection in Melbourne, which includes a large number of Greek vases, especially South Italian; next comes that of Phillip Adams in Sydney, which has a good deal of Egyptian, as well as Classical, material, and a particularly fine Hellenistic statue of Artemis. In Perth, the collection of the late Robert Holmes à Court contains a few Greek vases, and there are several important pieces of sculpture in private hands elsewhere (notably a head of Polyclitan type in Adelaide and a Tarentine grave monument in Melbourne). The time has perhaps come when an attempt should be made to produce a definitive catalogue of all antiquities in private hands in this country.

Classical and Near Eastern archaeology may be a relatively new discipline in Australia, but it will be clear that substantial progress has been made during the past thirty years in the development of university teaching in this field and in the provision of collections of original material which provide an essential complement to it. We are fortunate also that modern means of communication have enabled Australians to see several splendid exhibitions of ancient art, and there will undoubtedly be more to come. Further, the organisation of study tours to different parts of the ancient world has now become a regular practice, and this can lead only to a wider understanding of what antiquity has to offer and perhaps to stronger support for the development of our collections, which already give very tangible testimony to what enthusiasm, combined with a great deal of very hard work, can achieve in a comparatively short space of time.

Select Bibliography

The bibliography which follows refers only to general surveys or catalogues of the collections of antiquities in Australian universities and public institutions and does not include specific studies of individual items: most of these are listed by Frank Sear in *The Museum of Classical Archaeology: University of Adelaide*, Adelaide 1988, 22–5.

General

A.D. Trendall, *Twenty Years of Progress in Classical Archaeology*, Canberra 1979

Colin A. Hope and Jennifer K. Zimmer, *Ancient Middle Eastern Ceramics and Australian Archaeology in the Middle East* (Exhibition Catalogue, Melbourne 1983, with a series of essays on Australian contributions to ancient Near Eastern archaeology)

J.-P. Descoeudres, 'Australian and New Zealand contributions to the archaeology of the Mediterranean world', *Mediterranean Archaeology* 2 (1989) 1–8

R. Merrillees, *Living with Egypt's Past in Australia*, Melbourne 1990

ACT

J.R. Green with Beryl Rawson, *Antiquities. A Description of the Classics Department Museum in the Australian National University*, Canberra 1981

NSW

A.D. Trendall *et al.*, *Handbook to the Nicholson Museum*, 2nd ed. Sydney 1948

——'The Nicholson Museum' in *Art and Australia*, Dec. 1967, 525–37

Alexander Cambitoglou, *Classical Archaeology and the University of Sydney*, Sydney 1977

——*'The Classical Collection' and 'The New Gallery', Nicholson Museum*, Sydney 1978

M.N. Kelly, *The Museum of Antiquities: University of New England*, Armidale 1978 (NOTE. A catalogue of the A.B. Triggs collection of Greek and Roman coins, now in the Nicholson Museum, was published by Spink and Son Ltd, London 1924).

Queensland

D.S. Barrett, *Greek and Roman Coins in the University of Queensland*, 2nd ed. Brisbane 1982

M.G. Kanowski, *The Antiquities Collection*, Brisbane 1978

Bruce Gollan, *Classical Antiquities from the University of Queensland.* Catalogue of an exhibition held in the Brisbane Civic Art Gallery and Museum, 8 Nov.–6 Dec. 1982 (90 items)

J.M. Webb, 'Corpus of Cypriote antiquities in the Abbey Museum, Queensland, Australia', *Studies in Mediterranean Archaeology* XX.10, Gothenburg 1985

South Australia

Frank Sear, *The Museum of Classical Archaeology*, Adelaide 1988

Tasmania

R.G. Hood, *Greek Vases in the University of Tasmania*, 3rd ed. Hobart 1982

K.H. Waters, *Greek Coins in the University of Tasmania*, Hobart 1981

——*Roman Coins in the University of Tasmania*, Part I (Republic and Early Empire); Part II (Empire), Hobart 1981–2

Victoria

(1) National Gallery of Victoria (=NGV)

A.D. Trendall, *The Felton Greek Vases*, Canberra 1958

——*Greek Vases in the Felton Collection*, Melbourne 1968

——*Greek Vases in the NGV*, Melbourne 1978

P.J. Connor, *Roman Art in the NGV*, Melbourne 1978

References to the classical antiquities in the NGV will also be found in Ursula Hoff, *The National Gallery of Victoria*, London 1973, 123–8; Ann Galbally, *The Collection of the National Gallery of Victoria*, Oxford 1987, 71–9; Judith O'Toole, *Grecian Urns. Selected Vases from the NGV*, Melbourne 1987.

(2) University of Melbourne

P.J. Connor, "The Department of Classical Studies' Collection" in *University of Melbourne: Catalogue of Works of Art,* Melbourne 1971, 105–38

——'Greek Vases from the Geddes Collection on loan to the University Gallery, the University of Melbourne', *Iris* n.s. 1.2 (1988) 21–42

Antonio Sagona, 'Archaeology at the University of Melbourne: a short essay' in *Images of the Ancient World* (ed. A. Sagona and J.K. Zimmer), Melbourne 1988

STUDENTS, THE PUBLIC AND POTSHERDS

Max Kanowski
University of Queensland

In 1963 a Nolan amphora by the Harrow Painter was offered for sale in London at what appeared to be a very reasonable price. On making tentative enquiries the University of Queensland Classics Department was assured that the piece, though badly broken, had been skilfully repaired, and was an excellent example of its type. It was decided to ignore the taunts of uninitiated mockers who asserted that cracked pots are for 'crackpots' and bravely proceed with the purchase, a decision that was never regretted.

This first piece in the Antiquities Collection was soon followed by others, and inspired donations and bequests from University alumni, students and friends. There are now several hundred objects in the collection, together with a very large number of sherds.

From the very beginning it has been the policy to interest and involve the general public as much as possible. Items from the collection were taken on lecture tours to Central and North Queensland, the most valuable or fragile piece sometimes being carried on a lecturer's lap for the duration of the flight.

One of the most interesting projects designed to inform the culture-starved diaspora was a 'suitcase-exhibition' called Ancient Athenian Pottery in Craft and Art, containing a number of pottery items from the museum. Sponsored by the Queensland Arts Council, it travelled throughout the state to provincial centres, wherever the Council was represented, for two years (1983–4), and was designed to promote an interest in Greek pottery, and foster an appreciation of the achievements

"From the very beginning it has been the policy to interest and involve the general public as much as possible."

of the ancient world. The basic funding for the tour was provided by the Crafts Board of the Australia Council. To provide a background and adjunct for the display an illustrated booklet on ancient Greek pottery was prepared by Mr Bruce Gollan, the museum Director.

For a number of years the museum lent objects for the Brisbane Greek *Ekthesis*, a cultural display sponsored by the local Greek community. Our artifacts certainly attracted as much interest as the exhibits of modern Greek art and craft (painting, needlework, cooking), and in spite of being a static display managed to compete successfully with the dancing groups, who had all the advantage of music, rhythm, youth, grace and sex-appeal. During the summer holiday period of 1982–3 the museum lent a number of its finer pieces to the Brisbane Civic Art Gallery and Museum. About 18,000 visitors were registered as having viewed this exhibition.

Our holdings are now sufficient for us to be able to mount occasional special exhibitions in the museum. One noteworthy display was produced in 1985 as the Department's contribution to the University's seventy-fifth anniversary celebrations. It involved highlighting artifacts in the shape of animals, birds, fish and hybrid creatures. Special photography was used to enlarge the often very small decoration on gem-stones and coins, to bring them up to a size appropriate for public display.

The fairly liberal lending policy led to a couple of unfortunate accidents with fragile objects in the early years. Largely because of insurance problems removal of items from the museum is now discouraged. The newer showcases are very difficult to open without special equipment—another reason for leaving objects in position unless they really have to be moved.

School children and other groups are encouraged to book visits to the museum through the departmental office, where guided tours can be arranged. Until 1990 guiding was free, but a charge is now made to help pay for the employment of part-time guides. To give an idea of the time and work sometimes involved in this activity—recently a visit of approximately ninety students from Bundaberg required a succession of tours in groups of about fifteen that lasted most of the day.

"The Departments of Classics and Ancient History and Art History make use of the objects in the Museum for several courses."

Students are given a coloured postcard of one of the objects in the museum, and worksheets may be provided. Some schools prepare their own—often quite elaborate—questionnaires and work sheets. A typical sample produced by a history teacher from a local high school is three pages long, and contains sixty questions on such subjects as a Persian fertility goddess, an Egyptian shabti figure, a child's toy from Greece, and the wording of an inscription on a Roman girl's tombstone.

The Departments of Classics and Ancient History and Art History make use of objects in the museum for several courses. The exercise has proved very valuable for students taking courses with an archaeology component and courses such as Greek and Roman Art and Architecture, and Greek and Roman Culture and Civilization. The course in the Department of Art History that deals with the classical heritage has made extensive use of artifacts in the collection. More advanced students are asked to do research on the background and significance of newly acquired pieces, following the same sort of guidelines as they would have to use in preparing them for publication.

The Queensland University Education Department regularly requires Diploma in Education students to do assignments involving use of the museum. This is an excellent way of making prospective teachers aware of the potential in the museum's holdings for making teaching in Ancient History subjects more interesting.

The museum's holdings are strongest in Greek pottery and lamps. But there are good representative pieces for teaching purposes in terracottas, Greek and Roman coins, glassware and bronze. The bulk of the collection is relevant to Greek and Roman civilization, but there is also material from Egypt and the Near East. With the introduction of a new advanced course on Egypt in 1990 it is important to consider strengthening our holdings in that area. There is a particularly fine marble head of Aphrodite acquired in 1988 through donations from the Alumni Association. It is probably a second century AD copy of a Hellenistic original, and was formerly in the collection of Lord Clive of India. The museum has been enriched recently by being allowed to display several very fine Attic and South Italian pieces, on loan from Mr Geddes, a Melbourne collector.

University funding for the museum has been supplemented by a number of generous gifts from people such as Mrs Betty Fletcher, an Alumna of the Department, and Associate Professor Stanley Castlehow, who taught in the Department for over forty years. Professor Castlehow's bust, carved in Helidon sandstone, now looks out from the Michie Building which houses the musem. The carving was done by Rhyl Hinwood, a well-known Queensland sculptor, and shows Professor Castlehow holding one of the pieces of pottery bought for the collection from his bequest.

Some years ago the British Museum donated ten small pieces, and sherds were donated by the Museum of Classical Archaeology, Cambridge. The Department has also received a very substantial gift of many hundreds of sherds, together with some small glass and bronze objects and terracottas. The Corinthian and Italo-Corinthian sherds were studied by Joanna Savage, and many of them were published in the journal *Mediterranean Archaeology* in 1989. Her description deals with ninety Corinthian and Italo-Corinthian items, including pieces which are quite intact, parts of vessels which have been reconstructed

Bust of Associate Professor Stanley Castlehow on the Michie Building, University of Queensland. Sculptor: Rhyl Hinwood

from several fragments, and single sherds, rims and handles. The decoration on the vases, though sometimes badly eroded, is often interesting, e.g. a hybrid panther-bird with one outstretched wing. Some quite rare Corinthian motifs are represented.

"Students enjoy this close contact with genuine artifacts, and gain valuable experience for future work in archaeology or in museums."

There is still a good deal of work to be done on the remaining sherds (Italic impasto, bucchero, Attic black- and red-figure) and other material. Enough sherds survive from some pieces to enable sizable sections to be restored. Keener archaeology students are often very interested in contributing their sherd or two to the restoration of a piece, so having a small part in the solving of a fascinating three-dimensional puzzle. In practical classes students are given basic training in the handling, recognition, measuring and drawing of pottery pieces.

Several vases have now been restored temporarily to about two thirds of their original state, but may be dismantled and reassembled if other sherds turn up. Students enjoy this close contact with genuine artifacts, and gain valuable experience for future work in archaeology or museums. We have been fortunate to have in Brisbane a competent restorer, Miss Fiona Curtis, who has done excellent work on several vases.

In 1978 Max Kanowski produced a catalogue containing illustrations and descriptions of most of the museum's holdings at that time. Funding was provided on the understanding that the money should be repaid from income received through catalogue sales. This project paid for itself, but as fewer than one thousand copies were produced the catalogue has long been out of print. Steps have been taken to computerise the material required for a new catalogue, but shortage of funds has meant that the project is moving slowly. If money cannot be found to produce a complete new catalogue, it seems desirable to meet popular demand by issuing a small illustrated publication highlighting more recently acquired and more interesting and important pieces.

Coins are of special interest for the ancient historian. The museum holds a good representative collection of Greek and Roman coins from all periods, including a fine gold stater of Alexander the Great, a gift of the Alumni Association. The most recent description of the coins was produced by Mr Don Barrett in 1982. This is a revised and enlarged edition of his earlier catalogue, and contains descriptions of over one hundred and fifty coins, most of which are illustrated.

Some enquiries have been made recently about the possibility of combining several of the University's collections into a grand new building. This would certainly facilitate public access and would be very convenient for visitors. However, as there would be some loss of convenience for the Department, the reaction to the proposal has so far been mixed.

Our collection of antiquities, though conceived fewer than thirty years ago, is by far the most comprehensive in Brisbane devoted to the Classical world. For students it is a most important aid to an understanding of the past, while for the interested public it is a tangible example of our heritage from several ancient civilizations, especially those of Greece and Rome.

Bibliography

D.S. Barrett, *Greek and Roman Coins in the University of Queensland*, 2nd ed. Brisbane 1982

Bruce Gollan, *Classical Antiquities from the University of Queensland*, Catalogue of an exhibition held in the Brisbane Art Gallery and Museum, Brisbane 1982

M.G. Kanowski, *The Antiquities Collection*, Brisbane 1978

Joanna Savage, 'Corinthian and Corinthianizing pottery in the University of Queensland', *Mediterranean Archaeology* 2 (1989) 147–201

NEW LIGHT ON ANCIENT ANATOLIA

Trevor Bryce
University of New England

During the last 150 years, the ancient Near East has provided a rich field of investigation for scholars from a wide range of disciplines. Archaeologists, anthropologists, historians and philologists have all made substantial contributions to our knowledge of the ancient civilisations which rose, flourished, and fell in the land-mass extending from the Aegean coast of modern Turkey through Mesopotamia to the eastern frontiers of modern Iran. New discoveries of ancient sites are constantly being made. Some of these, like the site of Çayönü in eastern Anatolia, date back to the very beginnings of urban settlement in the Near East. Others of more recent origin provide evidence of highly developed political and social organisations, reflected sometimes in the finds of large tablet archives—e.g. at Hattusa and Kültepe in central Anatolia, Ebla in Syria, and Mari on the Euphrates. These written sources of information have provided a basis for research into the political and social history of the Near East, and important advances in the study of Near Eastern scripts and languages.

My intention in this paper is to discuss some of the major advances that have resulted from research into the ancient civilisations of Anatolia (modern Turkey), particularly those of the Late Bronze Age when Anatolia was dominated by the Hittites.

Hittite scholarship is a relative newcomer to the field of Near Eastern scholarship. Little more than a century ago, when important advances were being made in the study of the Bronze Age civilisations of Mesopotamia, the Hittites were regarded as no more than a small Canaanite tribe living somewhere in Palestine—a view based on a few scattered Biblical references. That picture has changed dramatically. We now know that the Hittites were one of the great powers of the Late Bronze Age, rivalling and eventually surpassing their two most powerful contemporaries, the Bronze Age kingdoms of Mitanni and Egypt. From their capital Hattusa in central Anatolia, they controlled a vast network of vassal states, which at the height of Hittite political and military development in the 14th and 13th centuries extended from the Aegean coast of Anatolia through Syria to the Euphrates river in the east.

In the early years of the 20th century, two important developments firmly laid the foundations for a comprehensive study of the Hittite civilisation, one of the newest and most important branches of Near Eastern studies:

(1) In the first decade of the century, the German archaeologist Hugo Winckler began excavating the site of Boghazköy in central Anatolia. The importance of the site was indicated by its size and impressive material remains, but more particularly by the discovery of large numbers of clay tablets *in situ*. Included amongst the tablets were copies of correspondence with foreign rulers. The most notable of these was a letter written by the Egyptian pharaoh Ramesses II and referring to a peace treaty which he had drawn up with the Hittite king Hattusili (III). This, combined with other evidence, made it clear that the site under excavation was the Hittite capital, later to be identified as Hattusa.

(2) While many of the tablets unearthed at Hattusa were inscribed in Akkadian (the international language of diplomacy in the Late Bronze Age) and thus could be read, the majority were inscribed in a language as yet unintelligible but clearly the principal language of the Hittites themselves. The task of deciphering the language was successfully undertaken in the 1910s by the Czech scholar Bernard Hrozný.

Yet with the decipherment of Hittite, called Nesite by those who wrote and spoke it, the many complexities of the field of Hittite studies soon became evident. From the tablets it was clear that Late Bronze Age Anatolia was occupied by a large, heterogeneous conglomerate of kingdoms, clusters of communities, and tribal groups that differed markedly in their size, ethnic composition and political organisation. The tablets range widely in their contents. They include annalistic records relating the achievements of the kings who composed them, political correspondence, treaties between kings and their foreign counterparts or vassal rulers, edicts, a collection of laws, ritual and festival texts, mythological and literary texts. From these texts we are slowly piecing together a fairly comprehensive picture of the history and civilisation of the Hittite world.

"With the decipherment of Hittite . . . the many complexities of the field of Hittite studies soon became evident."

Yet our investigations have thrown up many problems and difficulties—well illustrated by our attempts to work out the political geography of the period. The tablets provide us with hundreds of place-names—kingdoms, cities, villages, cult-centres, and in many cases the rivers, mountains or plains near which they lay. But the archaeological record provides us with locations for no more than a mere handful of these. And even when sites which can be positively dated to the Hittite period come to light, they seldom provide us with any worthwhile clues as to their identification. In most cases, we have to rely on information contained in written records in trying to localise the various countries, cities etc. to which they refer. Yet conclusions based on textual information alone must remain highly speculative until confirmation is provided by the archaeologist's spade. Every entrant into the field of Hittite political geography brings with him his own set of proposals and theories. It really amounts to what one scholar has aptly called 'the guessing game known as Hittite geography'.

Nevertheless, progress is slowly being made. This applies particularly to research on the political configuration of southern and western Anatolia during the Late Bronze Age. I have long argued, for example, that some of the countries belonging to the large ethnogeographical complex called the Arzawa Lands extended across the south-western sector of Anatolia to the region of Classical Lykaonia, Pisidia and Pamphylia. (See, e.g., my 1974 article.) Information contained in a bronze tablet recently discovered in Hattusa (discussed below) has indirectly provided strong support for this proposal.

Chronology is another problem confronting Hittite scholars. Unlike Egyptian records and the records of a number of Mesopotamian civilisations, the Hittite texts contain no official king-lists. Such lists can be of considerable value to the historian, in that they generally indicate not only the sequence of rulers, but also the lengths of their reigns, and in some cases the most important events and achievements of their reigns. Moreover, it is possible to work out many absolute dates in Mesopotamian and Egyptian history from the 2nd millennium BC onwards, given that the Egyptians and Babylonians kept detailed astronomical records for dating purposes.

This information can also be applied to Hittite chronology, whenever events in Hittite history can be synchronised with events in Egyptian or Mesopotamian history. Thus we know from Babylonian records that the dynasty of Hammurabi came to an end c. 1595 BC, and from Hittite records that it ended with the conquest of Babylon by the Hittite king Mursili I. Since Mursili was assassinated within a few years of his expedition to Babylon, we can establish an approximate date for the end of his reign. Similarly, we have a number of synchronisms between Egyptian and Hittite history. For example, we know that the military showdown between the Hittites and the Egyptians at Kadesh took place in the fifth year of Ramesses II's reign, when the Hittite throne was occupied by Muwatalli. According to the most recent revision of Egyptian chronology, Ramesses became pharaoh in 1279 BC. This provides us with a date of 1274 for the battle of Kadesh, one of the most important and most critical events in the history of Hittite-Egyptian relations.

In general, however, synchronisms of the kind illustrated above are quite rare. For the most part, Hittite scholars are obliged to draw what inferences they can from the internal evidence of the Hittite texts in attempting to devise a chronological framework for Hittite history. And the texts themselves do provide much useful information. From cross-referencing the data which they contain, we can draw up a relatively complete list of the kings who ruled the Hittite world, calculate in *most* cases the approximate lengths of their reigns, and attribute to specific reigns a number of the most important historical and political developments of the Hittite period.

But the task is sometimes complicated by the fact that a number of kings had the same name, and there is often insufficient historical information in the texts to enable us to distinguish between these kings. For example, one of the best known Hittite historical documents deals with the military exploits of a king called Tudhaliya, and is commonly known as the Annals of Tudhaliya. But there were several kings called Tudhaliya. One of them ruled at the very beginning of the New Kingdom in the middle of the 15th century, another near its end, some 200 years later. In the absence of clear evidence provided by the subject matter of the text, how do we determine to which of the two Tudhaliyas the text is to be assigned?

"Computer analysis . . . has led to some major rewriting of Hittite history."

Computer analysis has provided some assistance with problems of this kind. It has long been recognised that the Hittite language and script underwent a number of changes in the 450 years for which we have Hittite texts. And on the basis of the texts which can be firmly assigned to particular kings or periods, we are able, with computer assistance, to identify those features which typify the written language at a particular stage in its development. We can then apply this data, again with computer assistance, to texts of uncertain date—taking account of archaisms which scribes of later periods sometimes introduced into their compositions to give them an archaic flavour. This process has led to some major rewriting of Hittite history. Several texts traditionally assigned to the reigns of the last Hittite kings have now been back-dated 200 or more years—to the period of the first kings of the Hittite New Kingdom. Thus texts which have in the past been assumed to reflect the gradual disintegration of the Hittite New Kingdom in its final decades must now be seen as an indication of the weakness and instability of the New Kingdom in its early years.

One of the most difficult tasks facing Hittite scholars today is that of piecing together tens of thousands of fragments of tablets, which were originally assembled in the temple and palace archives at Hattusa, but are now widely scattered in various tablet collections throughout the world. Much of the blame for the extremely fragmentary state of Hittite written records must lie with the early excavators of the site, who failed to exercise the vigilance necessary to ensure that minimal damage was done to the tablets during the course of the excavations and to prevent illegal removal of the excavated material. Consequently, when a scholar succeeds in recognising that two fragments, perhaps in museum basements half a world apart, belong together, his achievement is often as important as the discovery of a previously unknown tablet.

A striking example of this is provided by the recent discovery of a 'text-join' to the document commonly referred to as the Milawata letter. The document has long been known, but originally only the left-hand side of the tablet on which it was inscribed had come to light—enough to tell us that in its complete form it contained important historical information, but too little to be of use for the purpose of detailed historical analysis. Then in 1981 Dr Harry Hoffner of the Oriental Institute, University of Chicago, discovered that a fragment in the Hittite tablet collection in Berlin fitted precisely along one of the broken edges of the document.

"We now have . . . information about a newly developing political structure in western Anatolia . . ."

In isolation, the fragments had little to tell us. But once the join was made, it was possible to start correlating the isolated, incomplete scraps of information, and to link up the personal and place names referred to in the letter. As a result of these correlations, the combined fragments have now provided us with one of our most important sources of information on the history of western Anatolia towards the end of the Late Bronze Age. I have discussed at some length the new contributions which the text join has made to our knowledge of political developments in the western Anatolian region in the mid to late 13th century BC—the period when the letter was written. (See my 1985 article.) We now have the name of a hitherto unknown king of the region, and information about a newly developing political structure in western Anatolia in the waning years of the Hittite empire—a structure of which we were previously unaware, and for which we have no precedent in Hittite history.

Recently, scholars have been turning their attention afresh to another longstanding problem of Hittite scholarship. In the 1920s, the Swiss scholar Emil Forrer claimed that he had discovered Homeric, i.e. Mycenaean, Greeks in the Hittite texts, on the basis of numerous references to the Land of Ahhiyawa in these texts. Ahhiyawa, Forrer argued, was the Hittite way of writing the Greek name Achaiwa, an archaic form of Achaia. And he noted that in Homer's epics, the *Iliad* and the *Odyssey*, the Greeks are regularly called Achaians. Forrer's claims were greeted with some enthusiasm, but also with a great deal of scepticism. Their most vigorous critic was the German scholar Ferdinand Sommer, who argued that Ahhiyawa was simply an Anatolian state, and that the resemblance between the names Ahhiyawa and Achaia was superficial and purely coincidental.

Since the 1930s, the debate has continued sporadically and inconclusively, with Ahhiyawa being variously proposed as an Anatolian kingdom, an island kingdom off the Anatolian coast (e.g. Rhodes or Cyprus), or indeed a mainland Mycenaean Greek kingdom.

Recently, however, an increasing number of scholars have come round to the view that the term Ahhiyawa must have been used in reference to the Mycenaean world, or at least to part of that world. The advocates of this view base their arguments on new readings and interpretations of the relevant Hittite texts, and on recent surveys of the material evidence for Mycenaean contacts with the Anatolian mainland.

While some scholars still have serious reservations about the Ahhiyawa-Mycenaean equation, the circumstantial evidence in favour of it is becoming increasingly persuasive. There is no doubt that Ahhiyawa was a major Late Bronze Age power, whose king was accorded by the Hittites a status equal to that of the other great Bronze Age rulers—the kings of Egypt, Babylon, Assyria, Mitanni, and of the Hittites themselves. Moreover, we know that Ahhiyawa had a substantial seagoing capacity, and was in close contact during the last two centuries of the Late Bronze Age with western Anatolia and the countries of the eastern Mediterranean. It is in precisely this region, and in precisely this period, that we have abundant material evidence for Mycenaean activity.

If the Ahhiyawa-Mycenaean equation is *not* valid, then we must accept that there were two discrete Late Bronze Age civilisations with remarkably similar names, making their presence felt in the same region and in the same period. One of them (the Ahhiyawan civilisation) is attested by abundant documentary evidence, but has left no identifiable trace in the archaeological record; the other (the Mycenaean civilisation) has left abundant archaeological evidence, but there is no identifiable trace of it in the documentary record. It is difficult to write all this off as mere coincidence.

Of course the Ahhiyawa-Mycenaean equation, if accepted, has substantial implications for Mycenaean studies, since to date the Mycenaean world has failed to provide us with any historical sources of information, beyond what can be gleaned from Homeric tradition and the Linear B tablets. And Mycenaean scholars, by and large, find it difficult to accept the notion of a Mycenaean kingdom with significant political and military involvement in the Near Eastern region. Certainly the equation poses many problems for Mycenaean scholarship. If Ahhiyawa was in fact a Mycenaean kingdom, where was the seat of its power located? At Mycenae itself, the kingdom of Agamemnon in Homeric tradition? Or at one of the other important centres of the Mycenaean world? If Mycenaean scholars are willing to entertain the Ahhiyawa-Mycenaean equation, it will be their task to consider the extent to which Hittite references to Ahhiyawa can be accommodated to a Mycenaean context. My own view (see, e.g., my article in *Historia* 1989) is that Mycenaean rulers had a far greater degree of political and military involvement in the western Anatolian region than Mycenaean scholars have been prepared to allow. This involvement had a substantial bearing on Hittite policy towards the west.

"The Ahhiyawa-Mycenaean equation, if accepted, has substantial implications for Mycenaean studies . . ."

Another matter which has received much attention in recent years is the Greek tradition of a Trojan War, the subject of Homer's epic poem the *Iliad*. Opinion has varied widely on the historical credibility of the tradition. Is it firmly based on fact, or is it purely the product of a fertile, poetic imagination? Many positions have been adopted between these extremes, as reflected in the large accumulation of scholarly and popular literature on the topic. However, most scholars agree that Homer's Troy did exist, and can be identified with the Late Bronze Age remains of the mound of Hissarlik, excavated by Heinrich Schliemann from 1870 onwards. And it is generally accepted that the region around Hissarlik provides a plausible setting for a conflict between Mycenaean Greeks and local Anatolians towards the end of the Bronze Age.

But if this region was in fact the location of an important kingdom during the Hittite period, then we might expect to find references to it in the Hittite texts. Forrer claimed to have found such references. In the course of his discussions of Ahhiyawa, he drew attention to the place-names Taruisa and Wilusa, which are mentioned together in the so-called Annals of the Hittite king Tudhaliya (referred to above).

These names appear last in a list of countries in western Anatolia which had rebelled against Hittite rule early in the New Kingdom (mid 15th century). According to Forrer, they were the Hittite way of writing Troia (Troy) and (W)ilios. Forrer also noted references to Wilusa in other texts, particularly in a well known treaty drawn up early in the 13th century between the Hittite king Muwatalli and a Wilusan king called Alaksandu, recalling the name of the Trojan prince *Alexander* Paris in the *Iliad*.

In spite of Forrer's arguments, many scholars have been inclined to dismiss the Wilusa-(W)ilios/Taruisa-Troia equation as improbable, or at best unprovable. One of the main problems with the equation is that until recently the Hittite texts gave no clear indication where the kingdom of Wilusa was located, beyond the fact that it was somewhere in western Anatolia. However, the discovery of a text-join to the so-called Manapa-Tarhunda letter has thrown important new light on this matter. The letter was written by Manapa-Tarhunda, vassal ruler of a western Anatolian kingdom called the Seha River Land. Scholars are in general agreement that this kingdom lay in Western Anatolia to the north of the region of Miletos. And it is now clear from the text-join that the kingdom of Wilusa lay *beyond* the Seha River Land, i.e. further to the north and in close proximity to the land of Lazpa, almost certainly the island of Lesbos off the north-west coast of Anatolia. There is little doubt, then, that Wilusa lay in the Troad, i.e. in the same region as Homeric Troy. This must considerably strengthen the possibility that the two were directly connected, if not identical.

"... it is possible that ... one of the conflicts ... provided a historical foundation for the tradition of a Trojan War."

Further, it is clear from the Hittite texts that Wilusa suffered a number of attacks during the 13th century, attacks which may well have involved, or been supported by, the king of Ahhiyawa, and which on one occasion at least resulted in the overthrow of the Wilusan king. If we accept that the Ahhiyawans of the Hittite texts were Mycenaean Greeks, it is possible that the conflicts, or one of the conflicts, in which Wilusa was involved in the 13th century provided a historical foundation for the tradition of a Trojan War.

There is little doubt that ongoing excavations at Hattusa will continue to bring significant new material to light. Indeed in the last few seasons of work on the site a number of important discoveries, including the remains of no less than 20 temples, have been made.

In 1986 a bronze tablet was unearthed in the vicinity of the city walls—the first surviving example of an inscription on bronze from the Hittite world; and unlike the great majority of clay tablets, the bronze tablet is completely intact, with some 350 lines of text. The text is that of a treaty drawn up between Tudhaliya IV, one of the last of the Hittite kings, and Kurunta, ruler of the Hittite vassal kingdom of Tarhuntassa. It contains important and hitherto unknown information about the royal succession in Hattusa, and provides a detailed boundary description of the Land of Tarhuntassa, listing the various countries, cities and rivers which lay on or near its borders. Tarhuntassa was an important kingdom of southern Anatolia, and became for a short period in the early 13th century the seat of the Hittite king himself (Muwatalli). The bronze tablet enables us to fix its location, in the region of Classical Cilicia and Pamphylia, and provides important information on the locations of other countries lying in its vicinity. I have indicated above that political geography is one of the most difficult and most frustrating fields of investigation in Late Bronze Age Anatolia. Particularly in view of this, we can hardly overestimate the significance to be attached to the discovery of the bronze tablet.

In 1988, the German excavator Peter Neve reported another major find at Hattusa—a built stone chamber embellished with a relief sculpture and a hieroglyphic inscription. The structure was associated with a Hittite king Suppiluliuma—probably the second king of that name and the last known ruler of the Hittite world. Suppiluliuma is named in the inscription, which records a number of the military achievements of his reign. In the relief sculpture a human figure is depicted, in priestly garb. Presumably this too is Suppiluliuma.

It is possible that the stone chamber is the actual tomb of Suppiluliuma. If so, then it is the first known royal tomb from the Hittite world. An alternative possibility is that the structure represents what the Hittite texts refer to as a ^{D}KASKAL.KUR—an entrance (in this case artificial) to the Underworld. The ongoing German excavations at Hattusa may help shed further light on this matter.

During the course of the 12th century BC, the Near Eastern world suffered a series of cataclysmic upheavals which were associated with the collapse of the major Late Bronze Age civilisations and the break-up of many longstanding patterns of settlement.

What happened to the Late Bronze Age populations? Were they displaced from their homelands, and if so where did they resettle?

These are questions which have engaged the attention of a number of scholars in their attempts to bridge the gap of almost 400 years which separates the collapse of the Bronze Age civilisations from the emergence of their Iron Age successors. Early in the 1st millennium, new languages, cultures and political organisations began to appear throughout the Near Eastern world, reflecting in a number of cases the introduction of new ethnic elements into this world. Yet in spite of the changes which marked the transition from Bronze to early Iron Age, many Bronze Age customs and traditions persisted in the new age. In some cases they were preserved by the remnants, or descendants, of indigenous population groups, in other cases by post-Bronze Age immigrants who absorbed within the fabric of the culture and civilisation they brought with them a number of the traditions of their newly adopted homeland.

The Iron Age Near East represents a blend of the old and the new—a blend clearly reflected in the large array of early 1st millennium civilisations—Phrygian, Lydian, Carian, Lycian etc.—which made their mark on the Near Eastern world before they in their turn slowly yielded to, and were eventually transformed by, the eastward spread of the Classical civilisations of Greece and Rome.

Select Bibliography

T.R. Bryce, "Some geographical and political aspects of Mursilis' Arzawan campaign", *Anatolian Studies* 24 (1974) 103–16; 'A reinterpretation of the Milawata Letter in the light of the new join-piece', *Anatolian Studies* 35 (1985) 13–33; 'The nature of Mycenaean involvement in western Anatolia', *Historia* 38 (1989) 1–21; 'Ahhiyawans in the Hittite texts', *Oxford Journal of Archaeology* 8 (1989) 297–310

T.R. Bryce, *Historical and Social Documents of the Hittite World*, Brisbane 1983

J. Garstang and O.R. Gurney, *The Geography of the Hittite Empire*, London 1959

O.R. Gurney, *The Hittites*, Harmondsworth 1990

H.G. Güterbock, M.J. Mellink and E. Vermeule, 'The Hittites and the Aegean world', *American Journal of Archaeology* 87 (1983) 133–43

J.G. Macqueen, *The Hittites and their Contemporaries in Asia Minor*, London 1986

M.J. Mellink (ed.), *Troy and the Trojan War*, Bryn Mawr 1986

M. Wood, *In Search of the Trojan War*, London 1985

WHAT WAS AN EPIC HERO?

Peter Toohey
University of New England

Before the novel there was epic. In most cultures it represented—and for how many millennia?—the most popular and, probably, the most practised form of literary entertainment. From the western steppes of Siberia to the littoral of New Zealand its popularity seems to have been unrivalled. The popularity has not been confined to performance. Epic is one of the most persistently discussed forms of literature. Books and articles focussing on Homer or on Virgil, to mention just two epic poets, abound. And quite a number of the best of these have been produced in Australia and New Zealand. What I would like to do in this essay is to look at one of the most basic aspects of epic—the role of the hero. The focus will be on Greek and Roman epic. Why the hero? It is a matter of origins: to examine the role of the hero is to examine the very nature of epic (even its 'generic basis'). And this is to examine the very heart of what makes literature compelling.

Can you have an epic without a hero? Certainly, if your definition is wide enough to include didactic or 'teaching' epics. In that case poems such as Hesiod's farming almanac or Grattius' verse manual on hunting with dogs or Manilius' astrological guidebook are all epics. But in the normal run of things—in mythological epic such as that of Homer or Virgil, or in historical epic such as that of Lucan or Silius Italicus—heroes and heroism seem to be essential elements.

The heroic impulse

Why did an epic hero fight? Homer provides us with one answer when Sarpedon meets Glaucus at *Iliad* 12.310–28. Sarpedon explains his motives for fighting as first, a desire to validate the esteem in which he and Glaucus are held by their Lycian people (12.310–21), and second, a craving to gain for himself some form of glory which will outlive his own life (12.322–8). That such an attitude did not prevail amongst his Iliadic companions is apparent. Anger, a desire for vengeance, vaulting personal ambition drive heroes such as Agamemnon or Achilles to fight.

The compulsion which impels the hero to battle has been termed the 'heroic impulse'. The 'heroic impulse' is an ambiguous affair. The motivations of Sarpedon are shown to be, if not productive, at least socially sanctioned. But when Achilles sets brutally to work in the

River Scamander (*Iliad* book 21) something has gone terribly wrong. Sarpedon and Achilles stand at two ends of a spectrum. The one character appears, within his violent world, as a humane possessor of a sense of shame (*aidôs*) and wisdom, the other as an over-reaching, destructive scourge. This ambiguity is not just a feature of oral epic. Literate epic also shows it. Consider Aeneas running amok in *Aeneid* 10, or contemplating the empty heroics of an early death in *Aeneid* 2. Compare his Achillean violence with the mercy he shows, too late, towards Mezentius' son Lausus at *Aeneid* 10.821–32. The varieties and the ambiguities of the 'heroic impulse' are central—it is almost a commonplace to say—for our estimation of epic heroes and epics themselves.

The sins of heroes

If all heroes were like Sarpedon the epic world would have been a far more civilised place. They were not. Perhaps it is just as well, for it is their heroic barbarities which often compel the narrative interest. The misuse of the heroic impulse is a persistent and, I dare say, a generic theme of epic. It is possible, however, to be a little more precise about the ways in which epic writers seem to have portrayed the ambiguities and misuse of the heroic impulse.

An epic hero is normally of superior social station, often a king or leader in his own right. He is usually tall, handsome and muscular. He must be, furthermore, preeminent, or nearly so, in athletic and fighting skills. This latter ability implies not just physical skills, but also the courage to utilise these skills. The epic hero is also sometimes outstanding in intelligence. Yet there seems to be more to the heroic character than is conveyed by such simple prescriptions. To display his heroic abilities the epic hero needs some form of a crisis or war or quest. The nature of this crisis and the hero's response to it seem to be at the heart of the matter.

The hero's response to crisis may best be illustrated within the Sumerian/Akkadian poem, *The Epic of Gilgamesh* (dating, in its earliest version, from the beginning of the second millennium before Christ). The hero of this poem, Gilgamesh, possesses all of the heroic qualities. The poem begins with Gilgamesh arrogantly alienated from his city. Here we have a hero who, to put it bluntly, has too little work of an heroic nature to do. He passes time ravishing the daughters and wives of his subject city, Uruk. Enkidu, a feral creature, saves him. The two set off in pursuit of warrior's glory, a glory which will outlive their lives. The heroic impulse drives Gilgamesh to fight the monster of the cedar forest, to kill a heaven-sent boar, and to log the cedar forest. But his selfish pursuit of glory alienates the gods. They cause the death of Gilgamesh's most loved friend, Enkidu. After a long period of grieving and fruitless wandering in the pursuit of literal immortality (even to the land of the dead itself) Gilgamesh gains some sort of a comprehension of his own nature and of his own mortality. He returns to Uruk and becomes, in some versions at any rate, a reformed ruler. He seems to have internalised the simple metaphor of the humane message of the old woman of Tablet 10: 'Pay heed to the little one that holds onto thy hand, let thy spouse delight in thy bosom! For this is the task of [mankind]!'

There is, in the Gilgamesh story, a simple pattern. At first the hero is at odds with his community. Personal tragedy, brought on by moral failure and subsequently accompanied by long wandering, allow him to gain a deeper understanding of his own nature. Having become the possessor of such virtues as loyalty, patience, endurance, empathy, and a proper sense of shame before his community and his gods, the hero returns to his people where he occupies his rightful place. To put it simply, the process depicted in the Gilgamesh story is one of personal moral growth.

Gilgamesh allows us to make more precise the tentative definition of an epic hero and through this an understanding of the inherent ambiguity of the heroic impulse. An epic hero will indeed be of superior social station and physique, he will be preeminent in fighting, courage and, maybe, even in intelligence. But, perhaps as a result of a quest, this hero will undergo some form of moral maturation. After being initially at odds with his human and divine community (misusing the heroic impulse) he will develop to gain a deeper understanding of his duties towards both groups.

Mythological sinners

What an epic does with the heroic impulse is what makes it interesting. Most epics treat the theme critically. There is a pattern by which the theme is outlined. This theme may well be a part of the epic 'genre'. The pattern may be detected in *The Epic of Gilgamesh*. It is also apparent in Homer's *Iliad*. Through Achilles (the Gilgamesh figure), we see an almost wholesale revaluation of the notion of the heroic impulse. How this is achieved is through the simple pattern of sin, alienation and final reconciliation—a process of moral maturation. When Achilles, in chagrin with his superior, Agamemnon, prays to his mother Thetis (1.407–12 and 505–10, cf. 18.73–84) for the destruction of his companions (in their destruction they and Agamemnon will recognise their need of him), Achilles evinces an extreme of alienation from his community. It suffers accordingly. But while Zeus may allow the substance of Achilles' prayer, he will not allow Achilles off scot-free. Achilles forfeits Patroclus (as Gilgamesh forfeits Enkidu) as a type of a payment for his prayer. Achilles, like Gilgamesh, must learn a sense of shame before man and god (and with this such virtues as endurance, self-control, patience, empathy, gentleness, loyalty, friendship and honour). When, in the final book of the poem, he meets the father of Patroclus' killer, Priam, Achilles finally perceives the importance of these qualities. In this scene Priam becomes, as it were, Achilles' own father. Achilles, as it were, becomes the man he has killed. Through this lesson of empathic transfer (compare *Aeneid* 10.821–4), the hero masters the virtues whose absence compelled his alienation. A proper reconciliation with his community flows from this. The process of moral or ethical maturation is at the core of the *Iliad*. Heroism and the hero, if not quite redefined, are understood on a more profound level than that offered by the simple definition of Sarpedon in *Iliad* 12.

Virgil's epic hero, Aeneas, learns much the same lesson. His progress represents an even more clear instance of the process of moral maturation. Aeneas, in Virgil's *Aeneid*, grows from the admirable, if irresponsible, aristocrat of book 2 to the mission-conscious leader of books 7 to 12. His growth represents a movement from a self-centred desire, if not for heroic renown, at least for vengeance against the Greeks, to a fully conscious acceptance of his fated responsibility: he must bow to the will and the plan of Jupiter and follow his mission to establish a new home for his gods in a Troy in the West (and incidentally to civilise the world). Like Gilgamesh Aeneas must become a good father to his people—but in accordance with the will of the gods. He does this, but not, it must be stressed, without considerable backsliding: in book 2 he almost throws away his life in the burning ruins of Troy, in Carthage love for Dido almost causes him to lose sight of his goal, in the fighting of book 10 he is impelled by a burning desire to avenge Turnus' killing of Pallas rather than by a resigned desire for the completion of his mission. In these instances the almost deranged Aeneas becomes alienated both from the plan of Jupiter and from his followers; he is barely able to conquer his anxieties and human frailties, and to continue with his fated mission. Reconciliation is not perhaps complete until book 12. In this book Aeneas has, in accordance with the will of Jupiter, taken on complete responsibility for the resettling of his people. The killing of Turnus, though a profoundly ambiguous action, does nothing to diminish the force of Aeneas' ethical maturation.

These three examples may allow a reaffirmation of the initial tentative definition.

Historical sinners

Epic, as we have seen, may be based primarily on mythology—legends concerning Troy, or Thebes, or the Argonauts, or Heracles. But it may also be based upon real history, utilising such themes as Rome's experience of war with the Carthaginians or of civil war in the last years of the Republic. The querulous Gnaeus Naevius (c.270–201 BC) wrote one of the first Latin epics. It was an historical poem: beginning with the mythological origins of Rome (c.1184/3 BC) it produced a narrative climaxing in the victory of the Romans over the Carthaginians in the first Punic War (264–241 BC). Even from the fragmentary remains of this poem it is clear that, rather than there being a single heroic focus, there are several. This appears to be the case for Naevius' follower, the Calabrian Quintus Ennius (239–169 BC) who repeated the process in his historical epic, the *Annales*, presenting highlights of the events between 1184/3 and 171 BC. Such an annalistic poem cannot have a single hero on whom to focus. The question raised by both epics is this: how can the hero and the heroic impulse be defined in poems so chronologically diffuse?

Naevius' and Ennius' poems exist in such a fragmentary state that from them clear answers cannot be had. There are, however, several later, complete versions of the historical epic which may allow more firm conclusions to be drawn. The best representative of this tradition is the *Punica* of Silius Italicus (AD 26–101). The seventeen books of this admittedly laboured epic recapitulate the subject of Ennius' poem, the second Punic War, but curtail severely the time-frame (Silius limits himself to the years 218–202 BC) and transform the style and outlook, which become in many aspects resolutely Virgilian. The narrative focus of the poem is divided, in the main, between two historical personages, Hannibal, leader of the Carthaginian invaders, and Scipio, the triumphant Roman general. The *Punica*, arranged probably into three incomplete groups of six books, blurs its heroic focus. It concentrates on Hannibal within books one to twelve, and Scipio within books thirteen to seventeen. Furthermore the moral contrast between these heroes could not be more pronounced. Hannibal represents a figure of demonic evil (1.56–60): a treacherous character, he has no respect for the gods or for human law. On the other hand Scipio, representing the ethical message of the poem, is the very embodiment of honesty, of respect for the gods and for human law (15.159–62). The moral attributes of Hannibal and Scipio are fixed from the beginning of the poem until its end. Neither character undergoes moral evolution.

Yet the heroic impulse is central to the *Punica*. In Hannibal's case, as ought to be apparent, the heroic impulse has been terribly misused. (One must admit, however, that Hannibal's heroic misdemeanours represent the most interesting passages of the poem.) In Scipio's case (and in a variety of other 'moral doublets' such as Fabius or Regulus) we have the very model of how the heroic impulse ought to be applied.

The theme of moral maturation, therefore, has been jettisoned, probably under the constraints of the diversity of the canvas of historical narrative. It is almost as if Silius has divided the stages of the moral growth of a single hero (such as Gilgamesh, or Achilles, or Aeneas) between two heroes. Hannibal, though driven by very different demons, could be said to represent Achilles in the River Scamander, Scipio (and his doublets) to represent Achilles at the end of *Iliad* 24. Silius, therefore, provides some indication of how the large-scale historical epic may have treated the heroic impulse. Because the time scale and the diffuse nature of the events narrated in the historical epic do not easily allow concentration on a single hero and on the moral growth of this single hero, the poet must broaden the focus. The heroic impulse, its abuse and its proper use are still at the centre of things. But the theme of moral maturation is transformed.

The same tendency is evident in the work of the Roman epic poet Lucan (AD 39–65). Lucan composed an incomplete historical poem (surviving in ten books) which describes the conflict between Julius Caesar and Pompey in the years after 49 BC when they fought for the control of the Roman Republic. (Caesar aimed at imposing his rule on Rome. Pompey intended to uphold the Republican tradition of rule by a senatorial oligarchy.) The time span covered by Lucan's historical poem is not as broad as that of Silius. Yet the characterisation of the hero within this epic is very similar. There is a blurring of heroic focus. No single hero is allowed to claim attention for too long: Caesar is too often absent, Pompey is killed off too early, and Cato is too often absent. Nor do the heroes undergo moral maturation. Caesar, Pompey and Cato, the 'protagonists' of the poem, are moral ciphers—the first illustrates utter and ruthless immorality (much like Silius' Hannibal), the second the deleterious effects of moral vacuity, the third the moral ideal of the Stoic sainthood (like Scipio). That these characters can be allowed no moral maturation is partly the result of the weight of ideas they must carry. But it is also the result of the breadth of the historical canvas.

The ambiguity of the heroic impulse, therefore, may occupy the same privileged position within the historical epic as it does within the mythological epic. Its abuse and its proper use are still at the centre of things. But the theme of moral maturation has been transformed. In mythological epic the single, narrowed focus allows depiction of individual maturation. In the more diffuse historical epic the process of growth is divided between two or more characters. It is evident, however, that a critical treatment of the heroic impulse is no less a generically privileged theme of the historical epic than it is of the mythological epic.

Conclusion

The conclusion is perhaps less important than the implicit argument. More attention needs to be paid to the generic characteristics of epic. Genre seems to condition not just language, situation and players, but also, to some extent, the ethical dilemmas faced by these players. My suggestion is that the nature of epic heroism is defined not just by physical excellence, but also by moral failure and often by subsequent growth. Such a conclusion may seem crude and insufficiently argued. (Perforce I have been selective. I have omitted the *Odyssey*, Alexandrian epic, and late ancient epic such as that of Prudentius or Claudian.) Yet the prevalence of this simple theme is hard to ignore. Perhaps the way forward is through comparative work. The conclusions ought ideally to be tested against the abundant 'oral' and 'literate' epics to be found in other cultures. Russian or Maori, Sudanese or Old English, the basis of these epics will perhaps provide an answer to the question of epic heroism and to the queries mentioned at the very beginning of this article.

What made epic so compelling? Why is it that we keep on reading and keep on listening to these stories? I have offered one simple solution: the enduring appeal of poems such as the *Iliad* and the *Aeneid* resides in part in their narrative and descriptive brio, in part in their ideas, in part in their language, but perhaps in even larger part their capacity to entertain enduringly resides in their satisfying depiction of the moral ambiguities of a great hero or heroes. The more extreme the ambiguities, the more appealing and the more satisfying the poem.

Further Reading

J. De Vries, *Heroic Song and Heroic Legend*, transl. B.J. Timmer, London 1963

D.C. Feeney, 'Epic hero and epic fable', *Comparative Literature* 38 (1986) 137–58

R. Finnegan, *Oral Poetry: Its Nature, Significance and Social Context,* Cambridge 1977

P.R. Hardie, *Virgil's Aeneid: Cosmos and Imperium*, Oxford 1986

A. Heiserman, *The Novel before the Novel: Essays and Discussions about the Beginnings of Prose Fiction in the West,* Chicago 1977

C. Martindale, *John Milton and the Transformation of Classical Epic*, London 1986

M. Mueller, *The Iliad*, London 1984

J.K. Newman, *The Classical Epic Tradition*, Madison 1986

K.F. Quinn, *Virgil's Aeneid: A Critical Description*, London 1968

R.B. Rutherford, 'The tragic form and feeling of the *Iliad*', *Journal of Hellenic Studies* 102 (1982) 145–60

——'At home and abroad: aspects of the structure of the *Odyssey*', *Proceedings of the Cambridge Philological Society* 31 (1985) 133–50

G. Zanker, 'Loyalty in the *Iliad*', *Publications of the Liverpool Latin Seminar* 6 (1990) forthcoming

GREEK DRAMA ON THE STAGE AND IN THE STUDY

Kevin Lee
University of Canterbury

I recently saw a production of Maxim Mazumdar's *Dance for Gods*. The play, written in 1980, portrayed the life of a fifth century BC actor who was a friend and devotee of Euripides. As a boy the actor had played the role of the child Astyanax in the *Trojan Women* and then as a man played Agave in one of the poet's last works, the *Bacchae*. Much of the play's interest arose from the actor's domestic circumstances and their reflection in his stage persona. But by far the most intense source of the play's energy were the short scenes drawn from the works of Euripides himself. The climax was reached with the finale of the *Bacchae*. The deranged Agave enters exultant with what she thinks is the head of a lion and slowly comes to see that she holds in fact the head of her son Pentheus, who had been dismembered by her and her fellow bacchants in their frenzy. Agave's change of mood and ultimate grief absorbed the audience totally, and this despite the simplicity of the production: a single actor wearing a plain white mask and a simple costume; a rudimentary set and lighting with recorded music as a background.

". . . there is a paradox which attaches to much of our interest in . . . the ancient world."

My experience could be readily replicated by theatre-goers all over the world before whom productions of Greek drama, sometimes adapted, are performed as a matter of course either live or in the cinema. Inherent in this response to ancient drama there is a paradox which attaches to much of our interest in and study of the ancient world: its abiding relevance in the midst of features which are profoundly alien. The actors in Greek plays make us shake with laughter or shudder with grief in a way so immediate that we are tempted to forget how foreign were the notions of the world, both theatrical and real, of the people who first heard and saw these plays in an Athenian theatre.

The audience who saw the *Bacchae* at the end of the 5th century BC sat in a huge open-air theatre, generating an atmosphere which is hard to imagine. For them a play was part of an annual festival held in honour of the god Dionysus and not simply a cultural event which might be repeated more or less regularly at any time through the year. They attended, of course, to be entertained and, in the case of comedy, to be amused at the expense of practically everything normally taken seriously and treated with respect; but at the same time they attended to be instructed: not in terms of some narrow programme, but by having their sensibilities sharpened and refined. The audience were no less aware of themselves than of the actors, and while present as individuals they were also attending as citizens, conscious that the dramatic festival was a state occasion, funded by taxpayers, and that the plays dealt with issues of importance to the community as a whole. In the case of tragedy, these issues nearly always took root in some episode from a traditional myth so that the plays satisfied the demand for both the familiar and the new.

The circumstances and expectations of a modern audience could scarcely be more different. Yet it is the response of an audience, or even of a class in a lecture-room, to these plays which shows that, despite its alien features, Greek drama has an ineradicable place in our own theatrical tradition and has conditioned in a unique way our notions of the tragic and the comic. The remarkable reception afforded the plays bears witness to a tradition fostered not only in the theatre but also in the work of scholars who attend to both limbs of the paradox sketched earlier: they attempt to recover as exactly as possible the historical reality of Greek plays—the precise wording and form of the texts, the details of the original production, the relationship of the plays to contemporary thought; they continually re-interpret the plays from their own point of view and thus ensure that they retain their vitality and are not condemned to a kind of *in vitro* existence. Australian scholars have contributed during the last twenty-five years to this international enterprise in a way which gives promise of an ever increasing understanding of the Greek stage as, to use the Maori term, 'a living treasure'.

It is worth stressing at the outset that the industry of scholars is not confined in its impact to the pages of learned journals and books of a forbidding appearance. Everyone would agree that Greek drama, so often sequestered in the study, needs the stage and an audience for its full realization. But it is easy to forget that modern productions and even the highly successful film versions of the plays—like those of Cacoyannis—are ultimately dependent, if they are to be authentic, on painstaking attention to the original text with all its ambiguities and interpretative possibilities. The study of the plays in university and school courses is now very widespread, so that, while those who can read Greek are in a tiny minority, the general level of familiarity with and interest in ancient drama among students has never been greater. The validity of these studies and the justification for this burgeoning industry rest on the quality of the translations available and on the guidance that goes with their use. To provide both we need an exacting scholarship which goes hand in hand with the ability to recognize what is essential and to communicate it in an uncluttered way. What may seem a basic query about an actor's movements or the tone and associations of a character's words may require for its answer very careful analysis not only of the text in question, but also of related texts and of studies in seemingly remote fields like archaeology and papyrology.

In fact, the bulk of the work done on Greek drama in this country has been of a literary critical kind. A Greek play was, of course, written for performance, and for the vast majority of the original audience a play, like a film or TV production today, had no other form of existence. But for us a Greek play is primarily a literary text and much of the energy of modern scholars is devoted to a close study of the poetic language in which it is composed, of the highly wrought form in which it is shaped, and, most importantly, of the structure and themes which inform the work as a whole.

"What may seem a basic query about an actor's movements or . . . a character's words may require for its answer very careful analysis."

Studies in this area have varied enormously in scope and focus. Alongside a lengthy and impressively detailed article on the characteristics of women's speech in the plays of Menander we find the late George Gellie's interpretation of all the plays of Sophocles in a book full of convincing insights which are the fruit of many years devoted to its subject. The study of Greek drama has a long history, and Australian scholarship is now part of a tradition dealing with seemingly eternal questions to which each generation of scholars brings its own answers. In 1977 D.A. Hester was able to append to an article dealing with the *Oedipus at Colonus* a bibliography running to some 200 items, which is, of course, already dated. A question may be ultimately unanswerable, but in attempting to answer it we are not simply engaged in maintaining the self-satisfying movement of an academic merry-go-round. Each new answer, if it is a good one, sharpens our focus on the issues, brings into play hitherto ignored or unknown strategies or pieces of evidence and, perhaps most important, relates our study of the question to what has gone before.

But while many of the questions we ask of the texts are traditional, some are quite new and arise from movements in related disciplines which impinge on the study of ancient drama in an indirect way.

We find, for example, structuralist and post-structuralist interpretations gaining ground in recent writing on tragedy. These approaches de-emphasise the individual, creative mind of the playwright, author of the text as an object with a limited and definite meaning; they see instead latent in the text polarities and ambiguities which are generally characteristic of society, language and patterns of thought, and which are not confined to the conscious aims of the playwright. In its more extreme forms the strategy can be decried as far-fetched and even self-indulgent word play. Its more discriminating use provokes an alert reading and an awareness of the fluid relationship between language and the reality it signifies; the critic's role is to expand rather than delimit the possibilities of meaning.

The fruitfulness of this approach can be seen in the treatment of the famous so-called carpet scene in the *Agamemnon*. Clytemnestra's deceitful and manipulative use of language to the ruin of her husband resists absolute definition. Its confusion of signification is open-ended and is itself a sign of the fragility of the system of conventions on which Agamemnon's power rests. It is not only his wife's verbal dexterity but also the challenge to the normal use of language presented by her words which foreshadows the king's demise.

Connected with this style of interpretation is what we can call the anthropological approach. Earlier generations were intrigued by the similarity of the Greeks to themselves; we are equally struck by the strangeness of their beliefs, their rituals, their moral values and their lifestyle. We are anxious to understand why they treated women as they did, and why they could pride themselves on freedom while at the same time making use of the labour of slaves. Such antinomies and tensions can be seen as the bedrock on which the plot and structure of the plays rest. The tearing apart of the king Pentheus in the *Bacchae*, for example, has been interpreted as a symbolic rending of the city itself, no longer able to contain within its political and rational institutions the refractory demands of the emotional and ecstatic.

But approaches both new and traditional which we bring to the texts are only as meaningful as the texts are reliable, and this leads to a consideration of the primary scholarly task: recovering as far as is possible the original wording of the texts. It is a curious paradox that at the very time when 'the text' as a definite document is being called into question, the editing of Greek dramatic texts is a growth industry. There is, of course, plenty of scope for the work. The words first spoken by Greek actors in Athens have reached us by a hazardous and circuitous route—Alexandria, Thessaloniki, Florence are typical staging-posts—which left them prone to wholesale loss. Even the surviving texts have suffered corruption at the hands of copyists and the lips of actors eager to expand their roles with lines either of their own making or transplanted from another source. Corruption, definite or suspected, is often significant for interpretation, and it would be wrong to suppose that editors are simply dotting iotas or crossing taus. A single example will make the point.

In one of tragedy's most famous moments the foreign sorceress Medea speaks a monologue in which she repeatedly weakens and reaffirms her resolve to kill her own children. The speech has been hailed as a masterful analysis of her wavering mind, and has long captivated both audiences and actors. The latest edition of the play excises almost half the speech as an interpolation and leaves us with something more coherent and generally tidier. The longer speech has had plenty of defenders, and may now be just carrying the day. The arguments are complex and of intimidating subtlety, but as long as the *Medea* continues to be staged and read, no one can claim that the issue is of merely academic interest.

The actors' words, we must remember, were only part of the performance, and the last fifteen years have seen an intense interest in the plays as theatre. This has, of course, both encouraged and been encouraged by the frequency of productions and by the growth of departments of drama/theatre studies in our universities. This field of study has been concerned with quite concrete questions of production: the shape of the theatre, costumes, acting styles and the use of scenery and props. Answers often seem tantalisingly vague, but in the absence of stage-directions we must generally rely on cautious inferences from the script. Beyond these concerns there has been the attempt to produce what has been called a 'grammar' of dramatic technique which aims to systematize the various norms which Greek dramatists seemed to follow in organising the speech and movements of their characters. This is not simply to serve the interests of all-embracing taxonomy, but to help us to interpret a particular scene by relating its features to the practice of the dramatist generally and to enable us to see more clearly how the scene is built up from a mixture of conventional and unexpected features.

Having discussed various approaches to the texts of the plays, we must mention the important contribution archaeology has made to our knowledge of the Greek theatre. Excavation of the ancient theatre sites continues, and our knowledge even of those sites excavated long ago is being continually refined. The finds of painted pottery that depict scenes which, it is reasonable to assume, are reminiscent of a theatrical production are of particular interest. Such paintings have taught us a great deal about costume and masks, and even, though here due caution is more than usually in order, about plays known to us only in name or by a few short fragments. In some cases the paintings deepen our appreciation of a scene by taking us beyond the spoken word.

For example, a late fifth century BC red-figure vase now in Malibu, California, has furthered our understanding of Aristophanes' comic technique. It has been argued that the vase depicts the chorus of the *Birds*, represented by two figures dressed alike: each wears tights decorated with dot-filled circles to which are added an erect phallos, spurs, a tail and wings; masks with a beak and a cock-like comb cover the head. J.R. Green of the University of Sydney has related this scene to the text of the play and shown how Aristophanes wraps words around the neutral bird-costume to suggest various species of birds

Malibu. The J. Paul Getty Museum 82.AE.83, Athenian red-figure calyx-krater decorated with a chorus of birds; after 415 BC. Diam. 23.2 cm.

known only to ornithologists with imagination and a sense of humour. It is precisely the sameness of the chorusmen's costume that allows for the witty descriptions which differentiate them.

The discussion of a text from a variety of positions is at its most engaging in a conference. In 1982 and in 1989 conferences devoted to the study of tragedy and comedy were held in Sydney and Brisbane. These attracted participants from the US, Britain, NZ and from all the Australian universities, and due attention was given to both the theatrical and textual aspects of the plays. In fact the dovetailing of the two was highlighted in the paper read in Sydney by an English director who regularly stages plays in the original language, and who looked at the question of a character's individuality from the actor's viewpoint. If we assume that the Greek stage does to some extent portray individuals, how is this conditioned by the circumstances of performance, in particular by the wearing of a mask? The stylization of personality to which the mask gives expression is effected also by the demands of dramatic form and the thematic movement of the play as a whole. But this does not mean that tragedy does not present us with strong individuals like Antigone or Electra. The actor must mediate between these positions, and it was precisely the attempt to define his role that stimulated close discussion of the text and its implications. Other topics too elicited a variety of approaches from people of differing background, ages and training, which made clear the immediate and abiding significance of these age-old plays.

Change in our society is so rapid that it is difficult to predict the directions which the study of Greek drama will take in the next quarter century. Technical progress will certainly make an enormous difference to our handling of the texts and to our attempts to define more exactly formal and semantic features of tragic and comic Greek. With the entire corpus of Greek literature available in CD ROM form, exhaustive, accurate and unbelievably rapid searches for words, singly or in groups, will make possible the more precise definition of meaning and the comparison of a wide range of linguistic phenomena from a variety of authors. Analysis of such data may allow us to make headway with some nagging questions, for example, that of tone, so vital to an appreciation of dramatic dialogue and so difficult to determine. Ready access to precisely all the relevant material may help isolate the associations of a word or word group and thus the tone of a given utterance.

There is even the possibility that the material itself may be augmented in unexpected and remarkable ways. Thirty years ago we saw in Sydney what can be called the second premiere of Menander's play *Dyscolos*. For a thousand years Menander, whose work has had a profound influence on our comic tradition, survived only in fragments and imitations. The sensational find of a papyrus copy of an entire play, on which a group of Sydney scholars did pioneering work, forced radical revision of many scholarly opinions, and gives the lie to the idea that Greek studies are confined to the Sisyphean re-working of the same old material. Other papyrus finds, though less startling than the Menander codex, have brought to light sizeable portions of new plays, including welcome samples of Satyr drama, a genre known otherwise from but a single instance, the *Cyclops* of Euripides. Discoveries of hitherto unknown texts are, of course, most exciting of all, but even the papyrus scrap of an extant play deserves attention, since it gives us a version of the text which antedates by more than a thousand years the mediaeval copies on which we principally rely. The latest edition of Euripides' *Phoenician Women*, for example, has the play begin with line 3. Recently published papyrus remnants of the play's opening omit lines 1 and 2; this suggests that the verses are not original, but crept into an early copy which formed the basis of the subsequent tradition.

"The sensational find of a papyrus copy of an entire play . . . forced radical revision of many scholarly opinions . . ."

New evidence, like new techniques, will certainly shape our studies in unexpected ways. But in the end the path followed by the study of Greek drama in this country will depend on the mood and taste of those who turn to it for enjoyment or inspiration or insights into the human condition. Scholarship will need to respond to these ever-changing demands while at the same time building rigorously on the knowledge accumulated in the past. This is a provocative challenge, of a kind not faced before. The work done during the last quarter century makes me confident that the next generation of Australian scholars will be equal to it.

Bibliographical Note

D. Bain, *Actors and Audience: A Study of Asides and Related Conventions in Greek Drama*, Oxford 1977

——*Masters, Servants and Orders in Greek Tragedy*, Manchester 1981

——'Female speech in Menander', *Antichthon* 18 (1984) 24–42

M. Dyson, 'Euripides *Medea* 1056–80', *Greek, Roman and Byzantine Studies* 28 (1987) 23–34

G. Gellie, *Sophocles: A Reading*, Melbourne 1972

S. Goldhill, *Language, Sexuality, Narrative: The Oresteia*, Cambridge 1984

J.R. Green, 'A representation of the *Birds* of Aristophanes', *Greek Vases 2*, Malibu 1985, 95–118

M. Haslam, 'Interpolation in the *Phoenissae*: papyrus evidence', *Classical Quarterly* 26 (1976) 4–11

D. Hester, 'To help one's friends and harm one's enemies: a study in the *Oedipus at Colonus*', *Antichthon* 11 (1977) 22–43

D.J. Mastronarde, *Contact and Discontinuity: Some Conventions of Speech and Action on the Greek Tragic Stage*, Berkeley 1979

F. Muecke, 'Playing with the play: theatrical self-consciousness in Aristophanes', *Antichthon* 11 (1977) 52–67

J.H. Quincey *et al.*, *Notes on the Dyskolos of Menander*, Adelaide 1959

C. Segal, 'Greek tragedy and society: a structuralist perspective' in J.P. Euben (ed.), *Greek Tragedy and Political Theory*, Berkeley 1986, 43–75

O. Taplin, *The Stagecraft of Aeschylus*, Oxford 1977

DEMOCRACY AND LEADERSHIP: AN ATHENIAN PARADOX

Robert Sinclair
University of Sydney

In 1952 *A History of the Athenian Constitution to the end of the Fifth Century B.C.* by the Oxford scholar Charles Hignett was published. Five years later Hugo Jones, Professor of Ancient History in the University of Cambridge, produced *Athenian Democracy*, which has been reprinted as recently as 1986. The two works may be seen as symbolic of two important strands in the study of Athenian democracy. One focusses on a constitutional analysis of the democracy, while the second focusses on the actual operation of the democracy and in particular the social and economic factors at work. The two strands are not mutually exclusive, and while investigations of the last three decades have tended to lay increasing emphasis on social and economic factors most scholars have adopted a comprehensive approach to the examination of Athenian public life.

Consideration of these various aspects is important in investigating one of the central questions of Athenian democracy and every political system in ancient or in modern times—the relationship between the people and those who exercise power or influence. By the mid-fifth century the fundamental features of Athenian democracy were in place, and in particular the sovereignty of the citizen assembly and the administration of justice by (comparatively large) jury-panels of citizens. Important changes were made at the end of the fifth century and during the fourth century, and the courts appear to have become more significant in a political sense in the course of the fourth century. These two fundamental features, however, and other features of the democracy persisted until the overthrow of democracy in 322, when the Macedonian Antipater imposed an oligarchic constitution, in particular a property qualification for citizenship.

In Athens in the period from about 450 to 322, the Demos (or People) 'ruled'. As one speechwriter declared in the middle of the fourth century, 'the Athenian Demos has supreme authority in the state and it is in its power to do whatever it wishes'. In the view of some, 'the will of the people' overrode 'the rule of law'. But Athenians, not least in the fourth century, were clearly conscious that the decisions of the assembly should conform to the laws of Athens. Indeed, the point being made by the speechwriter was that although it has supreme authority, 'the Demos has in its own restraint laid down laws to which it must conform if it wishes to grant anyone Athenian citizenship'. In all its decisions the assembly was expected to conform to existing laws. Indeed, any citizen could bring an indictment against any proposal (and the proposer), if the proposal before the assembly contravened existing law or was passed by an irregular procedure. The condemnation of the generals, who after the battle of Arginousai in 406 were denied separate trials as required by law, is a stark reminder that, in explosive situations, such constitutional safeguards may be swept aside, but the conclusion that this trial before the assembly was characteristic is not warranted.

The supreme power of the Demos was exercised, in particular, by the (adult male) citizens of Athens meeting in assembly. Some thousands of them—probably up to about 6,000—gathered together, usually on the hillside known as the Pnyx (about 400 metres south-west of the Agora). They decided the great questions of state—whether, for example, to go to war with Sparta and her allies in 432/1 or whether in 425 to treble the tribute collected from the members of the Athenian alliance. But the assembly also determined matters of regulation or administrative detail, tending to leave as little as possible to the discretion of officials.

"The supreme power of the Demos was exercised . . . by the (adult male) citizens . . . meeting in assembly."

A new procedure of 'lawmaking' introduced at the end of the fifth century has been interpreted by some as a diminution of the assembly's power. Yet the assembly discussed proposals for new or revised laws and the assembly made the decision whether to refer the proposals to the lawmakers or not. The new procedure is to be regarded rather as a brake on the lawmaking process, to prevent change such as the oligarchic revolutionaries had engineered in the late fifth century through snap meetings or stacked meetings. Moreover, it is probable that most decisions in Athens were the subject of assembly decrees rather than laws.

The comprehensive nature of the assembly's decision-making was matched by the determination to ensure that its decisions were carried out and that its authority was not challenged. The Council of Five Hundred (*Boule*), as Peter Rhodes' study of it has detailed, had clear responsibilities in supervising the actions of officials as they gave effect to the decisions of the assembly. Nor, as we shall see, were officials generally in any position to rival the assembly.

There were other parameters within which the assembly had to operate. In other political systems these might impose a crippling restriction on the initiative and authority of a popular assembly. The assembly, for example, was not able to make a final decision in a matter unless there had been prior discussion in the Council of Five Hundred. The council prepared the agenda for the assembly and members of the council presided over meetings of the assembly. But the specific arrangements in Athens meant that none of these provisions entailed serious limitations on the sovereignty of the assembly, while the council itself would have found it difficult to develop a strong corporate sense. For the council consisted of 500 citizens selected by lot to hold office for one year. A councillor could serve two terms, but not in consecutive years. The method of selection, the short tenure, the size and the changing composition of the council militated against a serious possibility of challenging the supremacy of the assembly.

Yet the very inexperience of many of the councillors might allow ambitious individuals to exert undue influence on the council. Apathy on the part of councillors, whether in attending council meetings or in expressing their views, allowed skilful speakers to manipulate the council or to dominate its affairs. That at least was the charge brought by Demosthenes in 355 against Androtion and his fellow councillors, and though we may suspect exaggeration on Demosthenes' part in pursuing the prosecution of Androtion, his allegations are not to be discounted entirely and perhaps reflect something of the reality of the day-to-day working of the council. Councillors who lived at a distance from Athens were probably less assiduous in attending meetings of the council: a resident of Marathon in the north-east of Attike would have taken six hours or more of fast walking to reach the city. Citizens with slender means, particularly those with no slaves, would have had less leisure and less opportunity to leave their farms or their usual occupations than wealthy citizens. In any case not all Athenians were predisposed to become involved in the public life of their city: the farmer depicted by Aristophanes as ready to pay his way out of being pressed into office was not unique.

" 'what was nominally a democracy became government by the first citizen'. "

We have, then, little clear evidence for challenges by the council to the authority of the assembly, though that may be due to the paucity of the surviving material. But there is ample evidence for individuals achieving a position of strong influence in public life. Two might be named by way of example: the young, flamboyant Alkibiades in the years after 421 and, in the 370s and 360s, the skilful speaker Kallistratos who was expert also in financial matters. Even more striking was the position of Perikles according to Thucydides: 'what was nominally a democracy became government by the first citizen'. That judgement referred, in my view, only to the last few years of Perikles' life and tends to obscure the vulnerability, even of Perikles. After his death political leaders were more on a level with one another, and their struggles to win the support of the Demos had, as Thucydides perceived, damaging effects on the Athenian war effort. Now the full implications of popular sovereignty which had been rather obscured by the strength of Perikles' influence were becoming more apparent. But even if his position was unusual (and there were those who derided him and his associates by calling them 'the new Peisistratids'—the new tyrants), the influence of individual political leaders in general is undeniable.

How was this possible? Such a position could not be achieved by virtue of the power possessed by a councillor or by most office-holders. Most officials had limited powers. Most of them were selected by the drawing of lots and so could not have the confidence of widespread support that popular election may confer. Most held office for one year only and re-election to the same office was not permitted. Most of them served as members of a board, commonly of ten. Above all, officials were 'accountable': at the end of their year of office they had to face a public hearing when any citizen was able to lay a complaint, and they had to submit financial accounts. Serious offences were brought before the popular courts. More than this, officials could be removed from office, and prosecuted, at any time during their year of office.

There were, however, certain activities which the Athenians believed should not be exposed to the chances of the lot and the risk of patently incompetent or inexperienced incumbents. For the use of the lot implied that all Athenian citizens not only had an equal right to hold office but also were capable of carrying out the responsibilities of office. Certain officials were therefore selected by vote in the assembly, and ambitious Athenians were likely to see in these positions opportunities for political advancement. These officials included the generals, charged as they were with the military security of Athens and Athenian interests by land and by sea, and, in the fourth century, certain financial officials, and in particular the Commissioners of the Festival Fund.

In a state which was rarely at peace in our period, the generalship was a key office. Even so, the term of office for generals was one year, but unlike the civil officials they could be re-elected. They served, however, as members of a board of ten. While they would appear to have been equal in power, individuals in whom the people had expressed their confidence by frequent re-election might be expected to have enjoyed a greater prestige and influence on the board. Perikles, for example, who was elected as general every year from 443 until his death in 429, must have enjoyed considerable influence on the board of generals in the last few years of his life. The generalship was, in terms of political influence, the most important office in the state in the fifth century and for much of the fourth century, and the endorsement of re-election or the appointment to command important expeditions would have been a potent factor in the influence of a Perikles not only with his colleagues on the board but also further afield, not least in the assembly.

"Some Athenians detected an envy of the tall poppy."

Like other officials, generals were accountable or responsible for their actions. If they failed to carry out the assembly's instructions or, on occasions, to meet the citizens' expectations of success, they could be removed from office and impeached before the assembly or the courts. Their fate might be death, exile or a crippling fine: some Athenians detected an envy of the tall poppy. Mogens Hansen's study of impeachment has demonstrated the grave risks faced by unsuccessful generals especially if they had lost the confidence of the Demos, though in estimating the likelihood of risk more account should be taken of the concentration in the evidence on periods and areas of special difficulty.

Personal renown as a general, however, did not automatically produce political influence. Athenian soldiers and sailors, it may be noted, were not full-time nor professional and their ties with their commanders were much less close than in many other societies. In the fifth century the general usually translated his personal renown into political influence by participating himself in the debates in the assembly. In the fourth century there was increasing specialisation in war and also in the art of public speaking, and generals preoccupied with military activity might seek the cooperation of *rhetores*. The term *rhetores* may be translated literally as 'orators', but it was applied in particular to citizens who spoke habitually in the assembly and the courts. 'Political leaders' or 'political activists' better conveys the sense of the word. Though they did not hold official positions as *rhetores* and therefore were not strictly 'accountable', they were subject to various checks. They could be indicted before the courts for making an illegal proposal, they could be impeached, their actions or their policies could forfeit the support of the Demos.

In short, the assembly constituted a critical arena for political power in Athens. For the assembly, as we have seen, was not hampered—or 'protected'—by a powerful executive nor by an entrenched bureaucracy. Nor was it restricted by an independent judiciary which is regarded in modern times rather as a check on the abuse of power by the executive or the bureaucracy and a safeguard for the citizens at large. In Athens justice in the more serious cases was mainly dispensed by panels of citizens, numbering commonly 500, but sometimes 200 and sometimes as many as 1,500 or even more. The jurors were selected by lot from 6,000 jurors, who were selected by lot each year from an eligible citizen body which fluctuated over our period probably between the low 20,000s and the low 40,000s. The use of the secret ballot in the courts and the fact that no appeal was allowed gave the jurors a sense of power and importance. Regarding the socio-economic composition of the courts and the assembly, the evidence is limited. In the 1988 volume of *Antichthon* I examined some indications which suggest that men of property were more likely to attend the assembly than the courts and that they constituted a significant element in the assembly, while the poor and the old may have been somewhat over-represented in the courts.

In both the courts and the assembly there was a directness and immediacy in decision-making. The decisions of the assembly were not considered by a 'house of review'. Proposals or decisions could be overturned or stalled by the indictment process to which we have referred earlier. This process was used increasingly about the middle of the fourth century as a manoeuvre against political rivals, and this abuse led to its devaluation as a serious check on 'unconstitutional' decisions.

This directness and immediacy of decision-making in the assembly and the courts enabled individual speakers to exercise very great influence. The assembly could draw on various sources of advice—the council, officials (especially the generals), commissions appointed for a specific purpose, individuals. And a leader of the Demos (*demagogos*) could and did derive his influence directly from the Demos. The secret of his influence lay in his continuing ability to persuade and in the success of his policies. This process of 'persuasion' on which the Athenians set great store was sometimes marred by appeals to emotion or by the pressures of the moment. The most notorious instance was the decision in 427 to put to death the whole adult male population and to enslave the women and children of the rebel city of Mytilene: in a rare example of second thoughts, the assembly changed its decision on the next day.

'Persuasion' was based essentially on the capacity of an individual, whether a general or a financial official or a political activist or a private individual, to communicate and to persuade his fellow citizens. Oratorical skill played its part. Political leaders sometimes charged the assembly with being at the mercy of their ears: those who did not have, had lost, or wished to win, popular support were prone to claim that the people had surrendered the control of affairs to a few *rhetores*. But critical too were the reputation of the speaker, his political intelligence and the acceptability of the particular proposal, and there is reason to believe that the Demos was less of an easy prey to persuasion than is sometimes supposed.

"The sovereignty of the people was not demonstrated every three, four or five years by elections or referenda, but was constantly and directly exercised."

It is this immediacy and directness of decision-making which more than anything else lies behind the paradox of Athenian democracy—the great influence of individuals despite all the devices we have considered. And despite that most Athenian of Athenian institutions—ostracism—which was of central importance in the fifth century, especially in the first half of the century. Every year the citizens had the opportunity, provided there was a quorum of 6,000, to send into exile for ten years any leader who was perceived as too powerful or divisive. The citizen inscribed the name of his 'candidate' on a broken piece of pottery (*ostrakon*), and the candidate with the highest number of ostraka went into exile. While ostracism was clearly a safeguard for the sovereignty of the Demos, it also had the potential to increase the influence of other leaders by removing one. Perikles would seem to have gained by the removal of his rival Thucydides son of Melesias in 443.

The sovereignty of the people was not demonstrated every three, four or five years by elections or referenda, but was constantly and directly exercised. In the process, the influence of individual leaders was great—and at the same time somewhat fragile. In one sense their considerable influence was to be expected. For the very structure of the democracy and the diminution of possible rival institutions involved, as Moses Finley argued, an inherent need for *demagogoi* to play an active role and to take initiatives. Moreover, as is clear from earlier, more aristocratic periods and from our period, Athenian society was highly competitive. Individual Athenians continued to compete strongly for political power and influence, but now in the changed circumstances of the democracy of the fifth century (and the fourth). Their fierce rivalry erupted in both the assembly and the courts. And, in the virtual absence of a public prosecutor, voluntary prosecution by individuals to enforce compliance with the laws made the vigilance and vigour of individuals critical.

Behind or around the individual there were networks of supporters. Recent studies have sought to go behind the leading individuals and examine the networks of supporters whose role tends not to emerge in the surviving literary sources. The ongoing study of inscriptions, the number of which has been significantly augmented by inscribed stones uncovered by the American excavators in the Agora since 1931, has increased our knowledge of well-to-do Athenians (reflected in John Davies' work) and of officials (reflected in the work of Robert Develin while at the University of Tasmania), political leaders and ordinary Athenians. The works of Robin Osborne and David Whitehead have investigated the activities of Athenians at the local or deme level. Mogens Hansen has published numerous articles on the democracy at 'national' level in *Greek, Roman and Byzantine Studies* and other journals, now collected in two volumes, and a synthesis of his views is to be found in his important book on the Athenian assembly. Of great interest is the advocacy by Greg Stanton (University of New England) and Peter Bicknell (Monash University) of voting by tribal groups in the assembly, while David Phillips (Macquarie University) is preparing a monograph on the history of the democracy in the last three decades of the fifth century. A definitive study of ostracism is much needed.

The endeavour to understand the complexities of Athenian democracy, and in particular political activity and networks, will continue, but here the last word might perhaps be given to the comic playwright Aristophanes. In the *Knights* produced in 424 Aristophanes explored the riddle of the relationship between Demos (portrayed as an apparently gullible old man) and political leaders (represented by his slaves). Throughout the play the clear impression is that in their fierce rivalry to win the favour of Demos the slaves (that is, the *demagogoi*) can manipulate and control their master. Demos however insists that though he has for long been deceived by their schemings, he shrewdly watches their tricks and their stealing and in the end gains for himself the benefits of all their efforts. The play ends with Demos now rejuvenated through the efforts of a new adviser and apparently in control of affairs. No doubt as they left the theatre in Athens in the winter of 424 the spectators were not unanimous in their views about the realities of the relationship between the sovereign Demos and the leaders who sought to exercise influence.

Select Bibliography

W.R. Connor, *The New Politicians of Fifth-Century Athens,* Princeton 1971

J.K. Davies, *Athenian Propertied Families 600–300 B.C.,* Oxford 1971

——*Wealth and the Power of Wealth in Classical Athens*, New York 1981

R. Develin, *Athenian Officials 684–321 B.C.*, Cambridge 1989

M.I. Finley, *Studies in Ancient Society*, London 1974

M.H. Hansen, *Eisangelia. The Sovereignty of the People's Court in Athens in the Fourth Century B.C. and the Impeachment of Generals and Politicians*, Odense 1975

——*The Athenian Ecclesia: A Collection of Articles*, 2 vols., Copenhagen 1983, 1989

——*The Athenian Assembly in the Age of Demosthenes*, Oxford 1987
J. Ober, *Mass and Elite in Democratic Athens: Rhetoric, Ideology and the Power of the People*, Princeton 1989
R. Osborne, *Demos: The Discovery of Classical Attika*, Cambridge 1985
M. Ostwald, *From Popular Sovereignty to the Sovereignty of Law: Law, Society and Politics in Fifth-Century Athens*, Berkeley 1986
P.J. Rhodes, *The Athenian Boule*, Oxford 1972
——*A Commentary on the Aristotelian Athenaion Politeia*, Oxford 1981
R.K. Sinclair, *Democracy and Participation in Athens*, Cambridge 1988
——"Lysias' speeches and the debate about participation in Athenian public life", *Antichthon* 22 (1988) 54–66
G.R. Stanton and P.J. Bicknell, 'Voting in tribal groups in the Athenian assembly', *Greek, Roman and Byzantine Studies* 28 (1987) 51–92
J.S. Traill, *The Political Organization of Attica: A Study of the Demes, Trittyes and Phylai, and their Representation in the Athenian Council* (*Hesperia* Suppl. 14), 1975
D. Whitehead, *The Demes of Attica 508/7-ca.250 B.C.*, Princeton 1986

THE SOCRATIC ALLURE

Robin Jackson
University of Melbourne

Ancient Greek philosophy was practised for over a thousand years, from roughly 600 BC to AD 600. From the time of his death in 400/399 BC the figure of Socrates rapidly became and thereafter remained the focus for speculation and theoretical reflection. Why did ancient thinkers care so much about the Socratic example? And why do philosophers and scholars today continue to care? I shall attempt to offer the outlines of an answer to these two questions.

The figure of Socrates came to embody the dramatic character and persisting interests of Greek philosophy.This development can be illustrated by the early emergence of what Aristotle called 'the Socratic writings'. Here a completely new literary genre arose—the reflective dialogue in prose, featuring a central character in conversation with his contemporaries—and concentrated on the exploration of the significance of Socrates' life, death and work. Plato and Xenophon are the best-known but not the only examples of this new genre.

Indeed all of the work of Plato, the most fertile of the Greek philosophers, can be seen as a series of critical reflections on Socratic principles. And Aristotle too, though younger than Plato and more distant from the urgent questions of Socrates' fate, regularly points out the relation of his own views to those of Socrates, especially on questions of ethics.

In the post-Aristotelian period, the philosophical concept of the wise man, the ideal of Hellenistic rationality, was explicitly modelled on an image of Socrates the wise. Zeno the founder of Stoicism, so the story goes, was inspired to give up his former lifestyle in favour of philosophy just by reading about Socrates. And when in the early third century BC certain philosophers took a sceptical turn, they sought to justify their rejection of claims to knowledge by invoking a return to the Socrates of Plato's earlier dialogues, who constantly asked questions but never claimed to find definitive answers to them. Even in the latest and scholastic period of ancient Greek philosophy, philosophers at Athens, Alexandria and elsewhere chose as their characteristic activity the writing of commentaries, typically on Platonic dialogues.

Not all of these later philosophers read the Socratic texts similarly or even equally accurately. Socrates' private life, for example, inspired very different sorts of imitation: there was the respectable behaviour championed by Plato and Xenophon on the one hand, and the riotous, outrageously anti-social lifestyle of the Cynics, such as Diogenes of the barrel, on the other. So too the variety of philosophical positions Socrates inspired was catholic. Sometimes he is adopted as the patron of pleasure-seeking, sometimes of an austere and ascetic way of life.

> ***"In our own day . . . Socrates remains arguably the most familiar figure from antiquity."***

But all these philosophers were nevertheless witnesses, in their different ways, to the centrality of Socrates and his example.

In our own day, too, Socrates remains arguably the most familiar figure from antiquity, and no course in philosophy or classics could claim to be complete without some examination of his significance. In recent years scholars have continued their painstaking analysis of Socratic argument. If the ultimate resolution of the puzzles of Socratic thought remains as distant and controversial as ever, scholars can nevertheless claim to have articulated them in a much more precisely and rigorously stated form. Like a classical symphony, each hearing of which reveals something one had not noticed before, so repeated readings of Socratic argument generate new possibilities of interpretation.

What explains this continuing appeal? Of the variety of Socratic texts the Platonic portrait has never been in doubt as the most powerful and philosophically the most authoritative. One might attempt to identify three elements in this portrait of Socrates, whose arresting character helps to explain his allure. There is first the invention of a distinctive philosophical method, the remarkable conviction that a process of critical questioning—logical demolition, as it were—could somehow construct a route to understanding and well-being. Then we might note the delineation of an ethical ideal: a vivid sense of the worth of a life of virtue, and the extraordinariness of Socrates' own commitment to it, even at the price of his own death. Above all, there is the fascination of the man himself, his idiosyncratic and novel lifestyle dedicated to the service of philosophical inquiry, his trial on charges of subversion, his execution.

> ***" . . . posing questions to all and sundry, expert and non-expert alike . . . "***

We might start with the Socratic method. The early writers confirm Plato's presentation of Socrates as one whose conception of philosophy consisted in posing questions to all and sundry, expert and non-expert alike, aiming to distract their attention from mundane concerns towards consideration of urgent issues of how to live. In Plato that process focuses on a search for definitions of familiar moral concepts, a search that never concludes successfully, but regularly ends with the rejection of candidates for definition. What such candidates typically lack, it seems, is a single account that applies to all instances of a concept and shows what is common to each of them. A proper definition would provide a standard by reference to which we can judge whether instances display the virtue in question. Lists of examples are insufficient: Socrates wants the single character they all share, and which, he insists, accounts for their being what they are. Socrates consistently maintains that he himself lacks knowledge of the definitions he seeks, the candidates for which he relentlessly eliminates.

Whether or not we take Socrates at his word—and reading the levels of his ironical utterances is one of the major difficulties in coming to terms with this figure—this is a distinctly odd procedure. How could posing abstract questions contribute to resolving decisions about how to live? And how could so apparently negative an approach to inquiry be thought to yield philosophical progress? One way of responding might be to note that Socrates' method presupposes that we need a certain sort of understanding to resolve our practical problems, and that being compelled to offer an articulate statement of one's grasp of moral notions is a test of that understanding. That same process seems also somehow to be a test of one's character, and submitting to a cross-examination to be the best route to virtue. 'The unexamined life', as he puts it, 'is not worth living by a human being'.

In practice Socrates' method consists largely in the undermining of firmly held convictions. As a result it is easily confused with purely destructive logic-chopping. Yet in its own idiosyncratic way it aims to be improving, embodying the belief that liberation from falsehood is a necessary preliminary for progress toward truth. This may be why, although respecting professional expertise in its own arena, Socrates vigorously challenges the idea that such expertise conveys any insights into general human well-being. Indeed he goes further: not only does he affirm the existence of a general understanding distinct from any special technical expertise, he suspects that possession of special expertise can tempt its owner into the illusion that no further insights are called for. That explains Socrates' otherwise paradoxical assertion that his own insight, namely of how little he understands, is, modest as it is, of more value when it comes to the big questions than the vastly greater technical discernment of the experts.

So we have a method that manifests itself in a determination to submit every thesis to a withering cross-examination and, if possible, refutation. This turns out, however, to be no mere knocking, but instead an inspiration to critical reflection. For his ruthless analysis of dogma in the light of critical reason aims to sweep away smug error and buttress the foundations of a truer understanding. By stimulating stronger thinking he hopes to strengthen behaviour. There is much that remains unclear in this method. Nevertheless its insistence on the positive value of a critical application of the intellect, in contrast with the employment of a purely instrumental or technical intellect, has great appeal, and is a distinction whose relevance to our own times is not far to seek.

If we move from his philosophical method to the second element, his ethical ideal, we encounter a similar summons from the mundane to the elevated: as he puts it, concern for one's soul is of greater significance than for one's body, by which he means values of a non-material kind in contrast to the prizes of everyday life. This summons is accompanied by an image of heroic optimism. For it seems to be Socrates' view that we are all of us—men, women, slaves, free—autonomous individual agents, potentially wise and good, motivated by rational desires alone, which are sufficient to outweigh other considerations in determining our conduct. This is in striking contrast with the more pessimistic outlook of his disciple Plato, in whose *Republic*, for example, psychic conflict between the promptings of reason and lower desires is central, and who notoriously recommends for most people rule by the reason of others superior to themselves.

For Socrates virtue is central to happiness: there is room for argument about the precise relation between the two, but it is clear that in his view the possession of virtue is sufficient for the good life. This was a vision whose practicality or otherwise became the occasion for heated debate among later Greek philosophers: does a good man necessarily enjoy the good life, for example, or are other goods besides virtue needed to complete happiness? Will the good man nevertheless be happy, even if denied all the other valuable things in life? Socrates' own position, while preserving the sufficiency of virtue for happiness, seems not to have been as extreme as the later Stoic view, developed from his own, which denied value to non-moral goods. Socrates does not reject the possibility, for example, that non-moral goods can be substantial, but he maintains that their value is dependent on virtuous use, and that in comparison with virtue itself their value is trivial. No amount of non-moral goods, that is, gives one a reason for preferring them to virtue.

Not only is possession of the virtues necessary and sufficient for happiness, but Socrates also notoriously maintains that virtue is unitary. The different virtues, that is to say, courage, moderation, wisdom and the like, are only apparently distinct, and should be understood as forms of a single virtue. What is this single virtue? As often, he does not say explicitly. But it looks intriguingly like understanding itself. For Socrates denies the possibility of moral weakness, the condition of knowing the best course but failing for some reason to pursue it. To Socrates such a circumstance is simply a failure of knowledge, a failure to see the good as it really is. Since by nature we all desire the good, he holds, it is only those who fail to understand it who fail to pursue it. So understanding is at the heart of his view of the good life. And yet he is dubious whether this understanding can be inculcated by teaching.

"Socrates denies the possibility of moral weakness . . ."

Now it is important to see that these Socratic ethical theses are not just arresting and paradoxical. Most importantly, they are defended by a thicket of argumentation whose weak spot, if any, is not at all easy to put one's finger on. In the hands of uninspired admirers, such as Xenophon, the fiery paradoxicality and wiry reasoning of Plato's portrait of Socratic ethics disappear, to be replaced by conventional moralising. But if divorced from its argumentative context, Socrates' ethical ideal can easily appear little more than moral earnestness, worthy perhaps but dull. For it is not just his call to values other than the merely material that is exemplary (though the application to our own times is obvious), but the relentlessly probing way in which he pursues these issues. He is not so much a preacher with an alternative vision of life as a critic armed with a battery of reasons to suggest that we already desire the course he recommends, if only we attend to his arguments.

This suggests that there is something about the man's character and personality that is relevant to his argument. And certainly the personal qualities of this figure account for much of his interest, not least his equanimity in the face of execution. His death, representing the suppression of free inquiry by a democratic society that prided itself on its openness, has been described as the great stain on the achievement of ancient Athens. Certainly its significance continues to be the subject of lively controversy in our own time. There seems little doubt that, although an active participant in Athenian democracy, Socrates expressed many theoretical reservations about it as a system of government. The unpopularity of such sentiments, at times when real revolutionary fervour was at a peak and when some of the revolutionaries had been among his associates, may have lain behind his indictment.

Socrates' critique of Athenian politics is easily caricatured, both then and now, as reactionary and anti-democratic. The truth, however, as always with Socrates, may be more complex than surface appearances suggest. For at the very least Socrates is far from a simple anti-democrat. Certainly he implies that if anyone actually possessed moral knowledge (a category from which he consistently excludes himself), then it would make sense for that person to rule rather than the many. But this opinion is heavily qualified. First, Socrates believes that anyone—male, female, free, slave—might qualify as such an expert, an openness alien to even the most democratic of ancient thinking. Second, although Socrates might favour rule by moral experts as a matter of principle, in practice he thinks there exist no such persons. For Socrates' utopian fancy to be realised, it would be necessary to transcend the limits of human nature. That is exactly what his disciple Plato develops in his *Republic*, but there is no evidence to suggest that Socrates himself advocated the adoption of such a system. And while he might praise

". . . Socrates' role is more that of a critic, who leaves us with interesting questions rather than dull answers."

the orderliness of political systems other than the Athenian, on balance the Athenian way, in particular its openness to freedom of speech, makes it the best available. His subversiveness, if that is the right word, is hardly that of a committed political activist.

I would suggest that Socrates' role is more that of a critic, who leaves us with interesting questions rather than dull answers. Sometimes, for example, he emphasises the importance of obedience to law; on other occasions, however, he insists that he would never obey a law prohibiting his philosophical questioning. Does he simply contradict himself? But he is someone for whom contradiction is abhorrent, and detection of it is his standard tactic. Or does he mean less than he seems to say in either case: that he does not advocate *any* resistance to authority, but resistance only under certain conditions; or that he does not advocate compliance with *all* laws, only those that meet certain conditions? Again, he does not choose to be explicit. Perhaps the very opacity and complexity of his own position is his legacy, a stimulus to others to explore his questions for themselves. Many have found his questions haunting, such as the Stoic Epictetus who returns again and again to the Socratic observation that a good man is immune

". . . a stimulus to others to explore his questions for themselves."

from harm. The Socratic example identifies something important about philosophical questions, that their inability to yield definitive answers does not detract from their importance or appeal. As he might put it, philosophy is searching rather than finding.

In identifying three elements—the fascination of the man himself, the delineation of an ethical ideal, and the invention of a philosophical method—I have given little more than a selective outline of some Socratic themes. But I hope it is sufficient to show that this is a complex legacy, one which it is as easy to misunderstand as it is to despise philosophy itself. It has given rise, in our own day as much as in his, to popular condemnation. But it is a legacy that calls for careful scrutiny, wherein scholars have an important part to play in rescuing the veridical and the inspiring from the cheap dismissal.

We speak of the man Socrates, as if reconstructing his thought were a purely historical problem. But Socrates is in fact much more a literary construction than a historical figure. Having written nothing himself, he is known to us only through his impact on the texts of others. But getting beneath the ironic surface of this figure is no ordinary historical task. For from his first appearance in literature Socrates' significance is that of a mythic figure, standing for a valuation of the worth of the philosophical life. The playwright Aristophanes, writing in Socrates' own lifetime, presented a comic Socrates of crooked and idle ideas. In Xenophon Socrates had become an exponent of soundly conservative opinion, no different in outlook (or pomposity) from other Xenophontine spokespersons. In each case, however, we can see the ability of the Greek imagination to clothe ideas in vivid and graphic guise, giving vigour to what might otherwise be lifeless abstraction. Just as the gods and heroes are memorable examples of Greek ideas on theology and valour, so too Socrates is a personification of philosophical ideas. In his case, unusually, we can witness the creation and growth of a myth, embodying the hope that human reason can be relied upon, at least in principle, to solve our problems and bring us wellbeing. Notice that this is not a myth in the sense of a fiction, but one in the sense of a powerful image, one whose potency remains intact two thousand years later.

Bibliographical Note

The popular (and unfortunately superficial) account of Socrates' thought and trial in I.F. Stone's *The Trial of Socrates* (London 1988) should be contrasted with the sober and substantial treatments of Socratic thought by Terence Irwin in *Plato's Ethical Theory* (Oxford 1977) and Gregory Vlastos in a series of articles, perhaps most conveniently accessed through his 'Socratic irony' in *Classical Quarterly* 37 (1987) 79–96. The long-running disagreement between Irwin and Vlastos has been as fruitful (and exemplary) a case of scholarly controversy as one could desire.

Australian scholars have also made distinguished contributions in recent years to Socratic studies, including Kim Lycos' *Plato on Justice and Power* (London 1987), Frank White's articles on Platonic epistemology and metaphysics, Harold Tarrant's work on the Academic tradition, and Godfrey Tanner's and Michael Dyson's articles on Platonic topics. One might also mention Peter Bicknell's articles on the Presocratics and Epicurus, and Paul Thom's work on Aristotelian logic. A contribution of my own to the complexities of reading Socratic argument is forthcoming in the *Classical Quarterly* of 1990.

THEATRE, PERFORMANCE AND PUBLIC IN THE ROMAN EMPIRE

E.J. Jory
University of Western Australia

Theatrical performances, or rather quasi-theatrical performances, were introduced to Rome as part of an attempt to appease the gods and dispel a plague in 364 BC. The association between stage performances and religious festivals and observances continued through the history of the Roman theatre. The theatres themselves contained shrines to individual pagan gods and it was this link between theatrical productions, sacred festivals and theatres which provoked many of the violent attacks on the theatre by the Christian Fathers. But while the origins of theatrical performances lay in religious observances, they quickly developed an important civic role as popular entertainment. As a consequence politics soon came to play an important part in the presentations.

In the second and first centuries BC aspiring politicians spent huge fortunes on lavish theatrical performances in extravagantly constructed if temporary buildings in the hope of winning popularity and votes to advance their political career and to demonstrate their affluence. In the late Republic the theatres, which had become one of the most important meeting places for the general public in Rome, became the site of demonstrations either in support of or attacking influential political figures of the day. The occasion for these demonstrations was either the entry of a political figure into the theatre or allusions (or assumed allusions) to contemporary political figures in the dramas produced on the stage. It is probably for these sorts of reasons that the Roman Senate had traditionally forbidden the construction of permanent theatres in the city of Rome until that of Pompey in 55 BC. However, two more Roman theatres were constructed a generation later after Augustus had seized power, and it seems clear that he and succeeding emperors used the theatrical shows to project their own image and test their own popularity.

In the provinces huge theatres were constructed in the first three centuries AD, in Gaul (especially in the area of Provence), in Spain and in North Africa. They were often built, with the encouragement of the central government, by powerful members of the local communities who thereby won favour with Rome and at the same time gained themselves local prestige as representatives of the Roman way. These theatres also contained portrait statues of members of the Imperial family ranged along the various levels of the high back wall of the stage, and so always in view. The magnificence of the theatre buildings, their decorations, and the elaborate provisions made for celebration of the games by political figures all make it clear that in the Empire as in the Republic theatrical performances provided more for the audience than mere entertainment—they had a political function also.

But to have any value as propaganda for Roman government the theatres had to attract large audiences. The aim of the research being carried on in the University of Western Australia, in collaboration with Professor J.R. Green of the University of Sydney, is to try to clarify what types of theatrical productions were performed in these great theatres and to determine among other things to what extent there was variation in the types of performances between the various areas of the Roman Empire. This in turn will help to establish whether provincial theatrical presentations were aimed at only Roman citizens, at Latin speakers, or at all inhabitants of the various provinces. It will lead to further evaluation of the political importance and the civilizing effect of Roman entertainment in the social life of the Roman provinces. In sum, it is to use knowledge of the performances as a basis for establishing a social and political history of the Roman theatre in the period of its greatest popularity.

The present state of knowledge

Close study of the literary sources indicates that very few full-scale performances of comedy and tragedy (that is, theatre in the Greek tradition) took place in Rome by the first century AD; the evidence is even more scanty for performances subsequent to that date. Evidence for such performances in the provinces is also rare in the literary sources. It is clear that as far as Rome was concerned mime and pantomime became increasingly popular and to a large extent formed the staple diet of theatrical performances in Rome. This literary evidence is supported by the epigraphic records which attest numerous epitaphs of pantomimes and some of mimes but almost none of comic and tragic actors. Archaeological data, in the form of objects depicting actors, their masks or even scenes from plays, partly confirm this picture but suggest it may be over-simplified; and for the Greek-speaking eastern provinces there seems to be a fairly clear suggestion that traditional theatre was performed until as late as the third or fourth centuries AD, even if as highly conventionalized productions of classics (analogous perhaps to some forms of Japanese theatre). In general, interpretation of this archaeological evidence is rendered extremely difficult because due to its nature it can give no indication of whether the performances of traditional-style comedies and tragedies were in Greek or in Latin, or whether they were in public or private. Nonetheless there is a firm basis for evaluating the monuments of tragedy and comedy since a methodology for this has been established for more than twenty years, Professor Green being a leader in this field. In contrast to this, while there are scattered references to monuments illustrating mime and pantomime, usually with qualifications about the genre, no critical methodology has been established to evaluate those monuments either generically or chronologically. The first stage of the present project therefore is to gather together the evidence for monuments illustrating mime and pantomime, to set up a photographic archive, and to establish a methodology for evaluating the significance of these monuments. This will be relatively easy in the case of monuments illustrating pantomime because the pantomime wore a mask with a closed mouth since he was involved in a silent solo dance performance. On the other hand, representations of mimes, speaking actors who were themselves maskless, are extremely difficult to define, and partly for this reason and partly because of a lack of interest in non-literary productions the monuments illustrating these types of performances have not received the attention they deserve.

Over the last ten years we have compiled comprehensive archives of the literary and epigraphical material (Jory) and of the dramatic monuments (Green). Our own experiences have indicated that the most promising collections of mime and pantomime monuments are to be found in the local museums established in the vicinity of large provincial theatres. The most extensive extant remains of Roman theatres in the West are in Provence, e.g. Arles, Nîmes, Orange, Vaison, Vienne, in Lyon, in Spain, e.g. Merida, Santiponce, and in the large theatres in North Africa, e.g. at Lepcis Magna and Sabratha. In 1990 we will visit the sites and local museums of the theatrical centres in Provence and Lyon to gather photographs and catalogue material. For this part of the work we are delighted to acknowledge an offer of assistance from Professor Ghiron-Bistagne whose local knowledge and expertise in the study of the Greek acting profession will prove to be invaluable. In 1991 follow-up research in North Africa (in collaboration with the work of Dr Sear's team from Adelaide) will increase the archive and permit comparative studies to be done, and in 1992, depending on results, an examination will be made of the material in one of the Eastern Roman provinces, probably at Ephesus or Miletus, to establish to what extent Roman theatrical tastes had been imposed or found their way into a major trading centre of the Eastern Roman Empire.

In the first half of 1990 work has been proceeding in Sydney on the identification, collection and interpretation of non-dramatic monuments illustrating theatrical performances in the Imperial period, while in Western Australia the concentration has been on investigation of the nature of the pantomime dance figures, the relation of this form of dance to earlier dance forms and theories of dance in classical antiquity, and possible interactions with the movements and gestures found in the contemporary danced dramas of the Orient.

A preliminary and very provisional account of the results of this part of the investigations may be of some interest, and may even shed some light on the way traditional drama was performed in Rome.

The nature and origins of the pantomime dance

The term 'pantomimos' occurs in Priene (in modern Turkey) in an inscription from the 80s BC and firmly connects the performers with the genre of mime. Pantomimes (in literary sources the noun always refers to the performer rather than the genre) were silent solo dancers who interpreted with movement and gesture a libretto sung by a choir to the accompaniment of a variety of musical instruments including flutes, pipes, cymbals, lyres, castanets and even organs. Each production, as in tragedy, was based on a story from mythology or history and, unlike a dramatic performance where the characters appear on stage together and interact, the characters in the pantomime were portrayed successively as the actor interpreted the roles in a sequence of interlinked but consecutive solo dances. The dancer concentrated on representing character and emotions, and the most important aspect of this art was the use of the hands and fingers. So dominant was the movement of the hands that the expression 'talking with the hands' became almost a cliché. This type of dance, as it was presented in the Imperial period, was known to the Greek writers of the time as 'the Italian dance' and perfection of the art is associated with two dancers present in Rome at the time of Augustus, Bathyllus and Pylades. Of these Bathyllus performed a type of 'comic' dance which quickly lost favour, but the 'tragic' dance of Pylades maintained its popularity for centuries to such an extent that the technical appellation of the pantomime on the epigraphic monuments of the Eastern Roman world was 'actor of rhythmic tragic movement'. Possible sources for this Italian dance therefore include the dances of Greek mime, Greek drama, Roman mime and Roman drama.

The dances of Greek tragedy

Despite the fact that the Greeks recognized the essentially Italian element in pantomime dance it was not long before Greek literary historians were claiming that the origin of this Italian dance was to be found in Greece and specifically in the dances of Greek drama. The first to make this assertion was Aristonikos, a contemporary of Pylades and Bathyllus, who provided the names of the specific dances, the Emmeleia of tragedy, the Sikinnis of satyr play and the Kordax of comedy. All subsequent writers seem to have echoed the words of Aristonikos with more or less accuracy and without, it seems, any question. But there are difficulties in accepting this hypothesis. The Kordax was a solo dance which was occasionally found in comedy, although it could also be performed by a group, while the Emmeleia and Sikinnis were dances of the choruses of tragedy and satyr play respectively and therefore would seem to be unlikely predecessors of the solo pantomime. Admittedly we have little notion of how the dances of drama were presented but the dancers rarely had a real dramatic role to play; indications of any sort of mimesis on their part, at least in the Emmeleia, are so scanty and subjective that some scholars have denied that it exists and there is no evidence to suggest that complicated hand and finger movements were a dominant feature. It seems at least arguable that the learned commentators of the Empire, misled by the similarities of theme between pantomime and tragedy, hypothesised a link between the solo dance of contemporary pantomime and the choral dance of classical tragedy.

Non-dramatic Greek dance

Mute dancing, a characteristic of pantomime, was by no means unknown to the Greeks. In fact it had been part of their culture from the earliest recorded times, appearing first in Homer as an acrobatic display where the dance as the Greeks called it was an individual rather than a choral performance, and at wedding celebrations. Acrobatic display together with a mute interpretative performance of a story is found in Xenophon's *Symposium*, and on Delos a nomos consisted of a chorus of boys singing while girls danced the meaning of the verses. The pyrrhic, a warlike dance, was originally almost certainly silent and imitated the movements of military training. The common ground of all of these dances is that they are not performed in the context of drama and dramatic festivals but outside them. Again we have no indication that finger movements played any major part in the performances.

Dance in Rome

According to Livy the earliest dance performances in the city were by mute Etruscan dancers who performed graceful movements to the tune of the flute. From the second century BC on even some members of the aristocracy attended dancing schools and took pride in their achievements as dancers although such expertise was frowned upon by the moralists. This dancing was undoubtedly solo but to what extent it was either mute or imitative we cannot say. It can scarcely have remained totally uninfluenced by the solo dances of the Greeks, particularly since the dance attracted Graecophiles like Sempronia, the mother of Decimus Brutus (one of Julius Caesar's assassins), a lady who became an expert practitioner. As in Greece, these solo dances seem not to be associated with formal drama although dance played a prominent part in performances of mime, and solo dancers, both male and female, regularly appeared in the theatres. Once more little is known of the movements of the dancers or whether the gestures involved precise finger movements.

We are on more certain ground when we come to the performances of comedy and tragedy in the early first century BC. In a long section in his work *On the Orator* Cicero speaks about the importance of delivery for the orator. Part of this is concerned with gesture and, while he contrasts the gesture of the orator with that of the actor, in doing so he makes us aware of the essential similarities. After speaking of the type of delivery necessary for emotional passages he goes on, 'But all these emotions must be accompanied by gesture—not this stagy gesture expressing the words but one conveying the general situation and idea not by mimicry but by hints, with this vigorous manly throwing out of the chest, borrowed not from the stage and the theatrical profession but from the parade ground or even from wrestling. *But the movements of the hand must be less rapid, following the words with the fingers and not expressing them*'. This use of the fingers seems very close to that found in pantomime. Although it is clear from the texts that Cicero uses to illustrate his point that he has in mind here performances of tragedy, there is no doubt that something similar was also done in comedy since all ancient commentators are unanimous that the comic actor Roscius was the supreme exponent of the art of gesture on the stage. The dance of the pantomimes was therefore in some senses an extension of a form of stage presentation already practised by dramatic actors.

Other possible influences

It is when we come to consider what these finger movements actually were that the possibility of a much less obvious influence presents itself. When Quintilian in his first century AD work on the education of an orator treats the matter of gesture he is very precise about how the orator should move his hands and fingers in different rhetorical situations. 'As for the hands . . . they are almost as expressive as words . . . the hands may almost be said to speak.' This is the language regularly used of the pantomimes with whom Quintilian must have been very familiar and although he, like Cicero, stresses the distinction between the gestures of the forum and those of the stage the similarities again are evident. What is striking about many of the gestures described is the uncanny resemblance to the finger gestures of Indian dance as described in the ninth chapter of the Nātyasāstra attributed to Bharata

Muni. The authorship of this handbook is disputed, and from our point of view unimportant. The date, variously placed by Indian authorities between the second century BC and the fourth century AD, is far too imprecise to allow us to make any suggestion as to the direction of any cross-cultural fertilisation, but the similarities extend beyond mere gesture to the nature of the dance itself. While there is great variety among Indian dance forms the basis is the Mantra, a mimed chant accompanied by a number of musical instruments, and illustrated by movements which include the 'nod, leg, knee, hand and spin' ascribed by Sidonius Apollinaris (5th century AD) to pantomime, but illustrated above all by movements of the fingers. A great deal of work remains to be done but it may turn out that the Indian influence on Roman life at the turn of the millennium extended well beyond the already known trading contacts.

THE DESIGN OF ROMAN THEATRES

Frank Sear
University of Adelaide

Theatres were important buildings to judge by Vitruvius who, in book 5 of his *On Architecture*, our principal ancient source, describes them immediately after the Forum and Basilica. They attracted innumerable benefactions as inscriptions attest. These took the form of restorations and repairs to existing buildings, embellishments such as statuary, or gifts of money for the staging of games. In some cases a wealthy benefactor would pay for the building of an entire theatre, as did Annobal Rufus at Lepcis Magna in AD 1–2. Such benefactions are particularly remarkable because theatres were among the largest and most richly decorated buildings in a Roman town.

Consequently theatres have attracted the interest of a wide range of scholars, including epigraphers, social and political historians, literary scholars, art and architectural historians, and of course archaeologists. Such is the pervasive interest in theatre that in a moderate-sized Classics Department like my own no less than three full-time members of staff pursue research in some aspect of dramatic studies. Professor Ussher has made distinguished contributions to the study of Aristophanes, David Hester has been no less active in his work on Sophocles and I myself have been involved in research upon the design of Roman theatres.

". . . theatre architecture imposed more severe constraints than most other types of building."

Theatres were extremely large and expensive buildings and it was usually essential, to save expense, that they take fullest advantage of natural geographical features such as sloping ground. Design could only be considered after size, site, and cost had been determined. Because the choice of site and correct orientation of the building are critical factors (Vitruvius warns against a southern exposure), theatre architecture imposed more severe constraints than most other types of building. Moreover architects were limited in their design options since the semicircular *cavea* (or auditorium where the spectators sat) had been universally adopted in the late 4th century BC. The geometrical limitations this imposed are all too apparent where the overall design

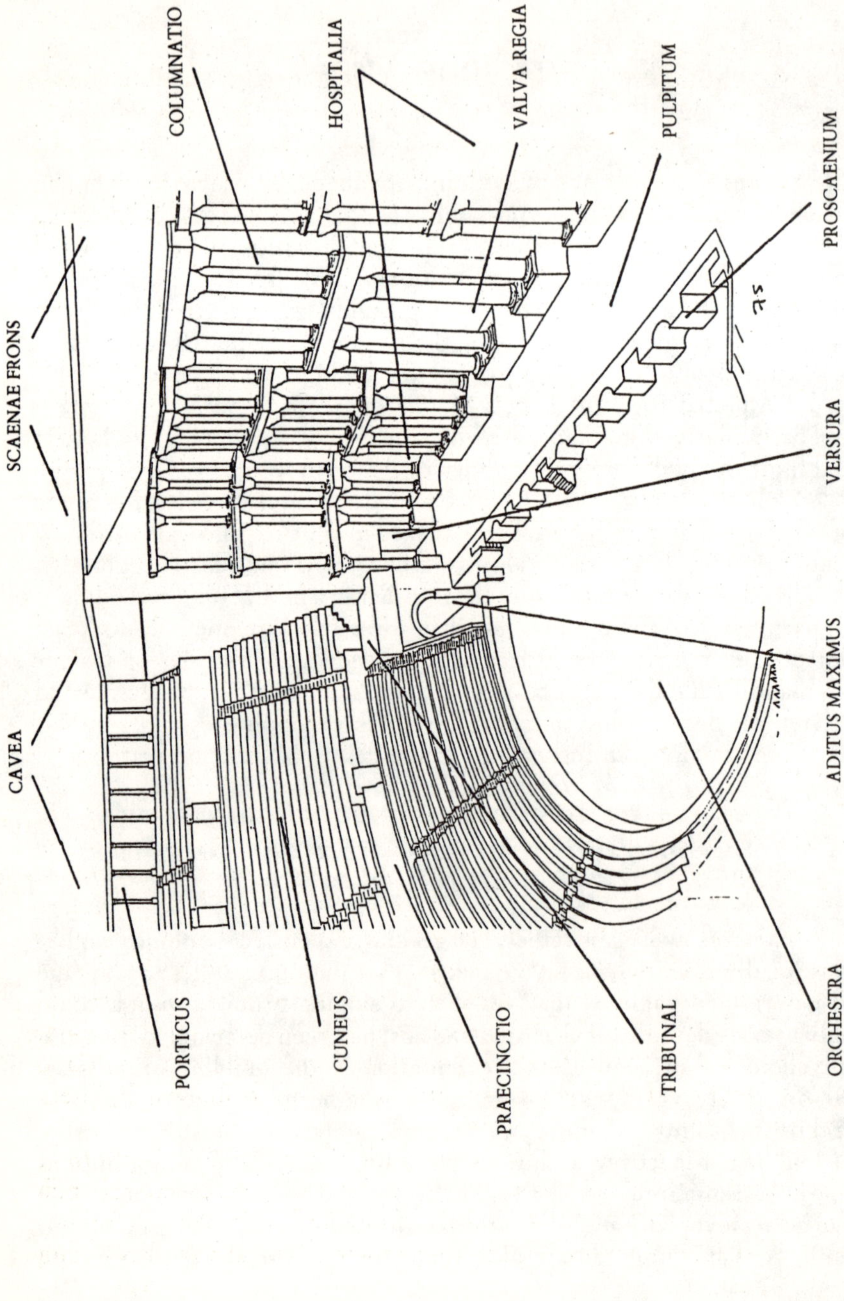

Diagram of Roman theatre

of the *cavea* and orchestra was concerned. The architect was allowed some latitude in the division of the *cavea* into blocks of seats (*cunei*), but the arrangements of the *cavea* were closely related to the arrangements of the stage and the doors through which the actors entered, as Vitruvius makes clear. The position and dimensions of the stage were in turn related to the size of the orchestra, as was the height of the *scaenae frons* (the back wall of the stage facing the audience). Scope for originality is further curtailed by the fact that theatres had an essentially practical function. There had to be good access to the seating by a combination of surface staircases and passageways and underground corridors. The slope of the seating had to be adequate to allow reasonable sight-lines. Another important factor was drainage, because the *cavea* by virtue of its shape tended to funnel rainwater into the orchestra. The stage had to be of a width, length and height such that the actors were within view of most of the audience most of the time. In the front of the stage provision had to be made for the curtain and for the workings of the ropes and counter-weights. Under the stage were the machines for turning the *periaktoi* (triangular revolving structures with painted scenery on them) and for activating trapdoors and other devices. Behind the stage rose the *scaenae frons*, a feature peculiar to the Roman theatre, which, being constantly in view of the audience, assumed a monumentality and richness far beyond the requirements of a place of entertainment. The wall could be over 20 metres high and be decorated with as many as three tiers of columns, more often than not of marble and sometimes over 100 in number. Between the columns were niches which contained an elaborate array of statuary. Above the stage was a sloping roof which deflected sound to the topmost parts of the *cavea*. As Vitruvius points out, architects had to be aware of the problems of acoustics, which meant that the seating had to be built to a uniform slope and that the roof of the *porticus*, a colonnade which ran around the top of the *cavea*, had to be the same height as the roof over the stage. Furthermore, rooms for the props and for the actors, as well as foyers for the audience, had to be fitted into the back and sides of the scene building. Finally, provision had to be made for the *velarium*, a huge awning which shaded the audience in summer and which had to be hung from a series of poles fitted into brackets and slots around the top of the building. The sheer logistics of catering for all these requirements and working within very tight geometrical limits clearly left a Roman architect very little latitude.

In no other type of building, with the possible exception of amphitheatres and circuses, were architects placed under such constraints. In the case of domestic architecture enormous variations were possible in terms of layout. Roman baths, although their planning was strictly subordinate to their function, show an enormous diversity of type and ground-plan, as a comparison between the plans of the baths at Thenae, the Hunting Baths at Lepcis Magna and the Southern Baths at Timgad, all in North Africa, will show. Although temples and basilicas were generally built to an orthodox plan, striking exceptions were possible, as the Pantheon and the Basilica Nova in Rome show. If such design latitude had been allowed in the case of theatres they would probably have been unable to fulfill their function. This is not to say that theatre architecture is dull and repetitious. Far from it. No two Roman theatres are alike. Each has its own characteristics, style and individuality, features mainly achieved by planning and design details, choice of materials, and sculptural decoration.

In planning a Roman theatre of the western type (the mixed and cult theatres of Gaul and theatres of the eastern type are excluded here) a Roman architect could make few departures from the established norm. The shape and divisions of the *cavea*, the relative size of the orchestra, the position of the *scaenae frons* and its three doorways follow a remarkably standard pattern for the first three centuries of the Empire. One is constantly aware of a strict master plan being applied time after time with few variations.

". . . the orchestra was the starting point of the design process . . ."

As Roman theatres are semicircular it seems reasonable to suppose that the design emanated from a single starting point. This seems to be confirmed by a unique discovery made in the theatre at Vienne in southern France by J. Formigé. A block with a pivot was found immediately under the edge of the stage in the theatre and it appears that the whole *cavea* was laid out from this point. Here one takes issue with Frézouls, who regards the orchestra of the Roman theatre as a 'résidu géométrique', a hangover from the Greek type of theatre where the orchestra had been a functioning part of the building. Clearly the reverse is the case and the orchestra was the starting point of the design process, an important confirmation of Vitruvius' rules for laying out a Roman theatre.

However the Vitruvian rules are a subject of great controversy among scholars involved in design theory. The reason is that much of what Vitruvius says about theatre design does not fit the majority of surviving buildings. The basic problem is that in most Roman theatres the *scaenae frons* does not lie upon the base line of the central triangle, as Vitruvius recommends, but on the rim of the circle which defines the orchestra. One wonders how far this discrepancy is responsible for the marked tendency, still current in the 19th century, to exaggerate the size of the orchestra in theatre plans. Even to this day archaeologists find it hard to accept the fact that their particular theatre does not fit the Vitruvian pattern, while the reverse tendency is evident in scholars who do acknowledge the problem. Frézouls concluded that while Greek architects planned their theatres on centrifugal lines, taking the orchestra as their starting point, to the Romans the diameter of the *cavea* was the determining feature. Hammond attempted to fit his theatre into the Vitruvian mould by a series of geometrical distortions, which succeed in the case of the theatre at Petra, but nowhere else. Small invented an entirely new design method which is ingenious but flawed. My own approach to the problem (Sear 1990) is to accept that the Vitruvian method was used by practising architects in the late 1st century BC, but that it, along with much else, underwent considerable modification during the Augustan period (27 BC–AD 14).

In order to test my theories on Roman theatre design, a programme has recently begun at the University of Adelaide to survey a number of important Roman theatres. One of the prime purposes of the project ('Roman theatres—an archaeological and architectural research programme') is to make accurate surveys of a number of important Roman theatres in an attempt to understand how they were designed.

"In order to test. . . theories on Roman theatre design, a programme has recently begun . . . to survey a number of important Roman theatres."

Accurate large-scale plans have been made of very few theatres, and in no case have they been made with an eye to recovering the design process. Although surveys and excavations over the last 25 years have greatly increased our knowledge of Roman theatre architecture, a number of important buildings have received little attention, for example the Roman theatre at Iguvium (Gubbio) in Umbria. This theatre is of critical importance because it appears to be early Augustan and may be the first known example of an architectural arrangement which was to become extremely common from the Augustan period onwards. Before that period both the *scaenae frons* and the columns in front of it (*columnatio*) were rectilinear, but early in the Augustan period a more animated design appeared, with the central doorway (*valva regia*) enclosed in a curved niche and the lateral doorways (*hospitalia*) enclosed in shallow rectangular niches. The architectural fragments from the *scaenae frons*, which are now housed in the Palazzo dei Consoli, suggest that the theatre at Gubbio must have been one of the earliest to have its *scaenae frons* laid out in this way. The Adelaide team has obtained permission to work on this important theatre and began its first season in June 1990. The aims of the project are to produce an accurate survey of the theatre with a view firstly to testing the theory I have proposed as to how Roman theatres were designed (Sear 1990); secondly to confirm the date of the building by analysis of its masonry and the surviving architectural ornament; thirdly to attempt a restoration, on paper, of the original appearance of the theatre, especially the *scaenae frons* (if this proves feasible given the scanty amount of evidence surviving). This last aim is particularly important because existing restorations are unconvincing.

The team would also like to study a number of theatres in North Africa. The theatres at Ammaedara (Haïdra), Simitthu (Chemtou) and Sufetula (Sbeitla), all in Tunisia, need further documentation and are important in North African theatre history. The large theatre at Carthage also needs further study, as do the theatres at Bulla Regia and Cillium (Kasserine). In the case of the latter an attempted restoration of the *scaenae frons* is highly improbable, but only on-the-spot research can clarify the position. The Hadrianic theatre at Carthage and the Antonine theatre at Bulla Regia are of interest because they both have all three doorways of the *scaenae frons* enclosed in curved niches. This was a feature of many North African theatres of the 2nd and early 3rd century AD. Other examples are the theatre at Lepcis Magna whose *scaenae frons* was rebuilt in Antonine times, the Severan theatre at Sabratha, the late 2nd or early 3rd century AD theatre at Thubursicu Numidarum, and the early 3rd century AD theatre at Madauros.

Another theatre which the team intends to study is the theatre at Taormina in Sicily. This large, well-preserved building has never been properly surveyed. A careful study of the building may reveal important information about the arrangements of its *scaenae frons* and the late-antique transformation of the orchestra into an arena. Stylistic comparisons may well confirm that it is akin, not to theatres of North Africa as has been maintained, but to theatres of the eastern Empire.

The team intends to work co-operatively with the team from the Universities of Sydney and Western Australia headed by Professor J.R. Green and Professor E.J. Jory who are studying aspects of theatrical performance. I have already collaborated with Professor Jory in theatre research and we hope that some aspects of our work will be published jointly. One particular aspect of theatre studies which will profit from a collaborative approach is the interpretation of theatre inscriptions. A plan is at present afoot for the two teams to join forces in Tunisia in 1991.

The Adelaide project, which has been supported by an Australian Research Council grant, is expected to take some five to six years to complete. Fortunately we have advanced surveying equipment and excellent photographic equipment, indispensable items for high quality documentation. But, most important of all, we have a first-class team of draughtsmen. Our architects, Zig Kapelis and Barry Rowney, from the Department of Architecture in the University of Adelaide, have worked with ancient monuments for many years and both have had considerable experience working for the Australian Expedition to Pompeii (see the article by G.W. Clarke above). In the 1990 campaign we will as usual have a number of volunteers and one research student will work in association with the team. I am confident that the documentation the team will produce will be of a high standard and will fill valuable gaps in the published record of Roman theatres. I hope too that our results will elucidate some of the more complex aspects of Roman theatre design.

Recent work on Roman theatres

Much attention has recently focussed upon the origins of the Roman type of theatre. Useful contributions to the debate are by H. Lauter and by H.P. Isler, whose work deals particularly with the connections between the Hellenistic theatre in Sicily and the theatres of Campania. The recent discovery of a 4th century BC theatre at Metapontum and its excavation by D. Mertens also has important implications for the history of the Roman theatre.

A number of monographs on important individual theatres have appeared over the last few years. The latest is by G. Caputo on the theatre at Lepcis Magna, which will now join the growing list of important North African theatres which have finally received detailed documentation. These include the theatre at Sabratha (also published by Caputo), the largest North African theatre, that at Carthage, and the theatre at Bulla Regia. The most recent book on the theatres of North Africa, by Lachaux, is a valuable one, although it lacks ground-plans.

Several important theatres in France have long since been documented and good plans are available of the theatres at Lyon, Vaison and Vienne. Unfortunately no complete detailed plan has been published of the important theatre at Orange and measured details of its *scaenae frons* are lacking. In Spain on the other hand an important work has recently been published which provides extensive documentation and plans of fifteen theatres in the Iberian peninsula.

In Syria only a small number of theatres have been fully documented, such as the theatres at Caesarea, Petra, Philippopolis, Beth-Shean and Bosra.

Comprehensive works are available on the theatres of Asia Minor and Yugoslavia, but in Italy progress has been patchy, although several attempts have been made to initiate a Corpus Theatrorum Italicorum or Antiquorum. However several major theatres have been fully documented in the last few years, notably Syracuse, Saepinum, Aosta, Turin and Ferento. Recent studies have added much to our knowledge of the important theatre at Volterra (published in 1955 without a groundplan), Brescia and Luni.

A number of recent works deal with particular aspects of theatre buildings, such as the workings of the *velarium* and sculptural decoration.

Bibliography

M. Bieber, *The History of the Greek and Roman Theater*, Princeton 1961

E. Frézouls, 'Aspects de l'histoire architecturale du théâtre romain', *Aufstieg und Niedergang der römischen Welt* 12.2 (Berlin 1982) 343–441

P.C. Hammond, *The Excavation of the Main Theater at Petra*, London 1965

F.B. Sear, 'Vitruvius and Roman theater design', *American Journal of Archaeology* 94 (1990) 249–58

D.B. Small, 'Studies in Roman theater design', *American Journal of Archaeology* 87 (1983) 55–68

THE FAMILY

Beryl Rawson
Australian National University

We all belong to a family, in one sense or another, so we all think we know what a 'family' is. But this apparently solid concept fragments into a variety of different-coloured prisms as soon as we train the academic microscope on it, and sometimes the pieces re-form into new combinations and shapes and colours as we change the focus and examine it from different perspectives. 'The family' now engages the interest of many disciplines—anthropology, demography, history, law, psychology, sociology (amongst others): a reflection of the central role which the family has played in most societies, and a response to the complexity and variety of that role. 'The family' has become a major growth area in classical studies, and it is precisely the interdisciplinary nature of Classics and Ancient History which has made this field so productive and so stimulating.

" 'The family' now engages the interest of many disciplines . . . "

Roman historians have long been in the forefront of family studies in one particular way. Earlier this century they saw the importance of the family in Roman political history. As Roman politics were not based on the modern party system, family connections were used to explain many of the unions (and disunions) of Roman public life. The flourishing sub-discipline of 'prosopography' developed, in which family histories and connections were reconstructed in great detail. Although some historians now distance themselves from the extreme claims of the prosopographical approach, the importance of the family (of birth and by marriage) is still widely acknowledged for public life in the Republican and Empire periods (especially the last century BC and the first two centuries AD).

It is in the last two or three decades that the new phase of family studies has taken off, attracting younger scholars who have seen the possibilities in the approaches of the newer disciplines, in the use of the computer, in the new 'sciences' which are unlocking old evidence, e.g. epigraphy (inscriptions) and numismatics (coins), and in a more socially focussed approach to law and archaeology. Australian and New Zealand scholars have played an important part in these developments. The first international conference on 'The Roman family' was held in Canberra in 1981, and a second one—in 1988—was attended by scholars from Canada, the United States, England, France and Belgium as well as from Australia and New Zealand.

One of the difficulties in studying the ancient Greeks and Romans is the nature and quantity of the sources available. Much has been lost and much of what remains is 'high literature'—written by, for and (largely) about high society. All pre-modern societies have left little by way of census data and other systematic statistics, or by way of personal memoirs of women, children, servants and slaves; we are thus limited in our ability to quantify, to trace developments, and to discuss the more private aspects of family life in these societies. Nevertheless, new methodologies have been developed and new material exploited in recent years to extend the boundaries of our knowledge and understanding of family and household in earlier societies. The Cambridge Group for the History of Population and Social Structure did pioneering work for post-medieval English and Western European societies, using particularly parish records. Linda Pollock analysed primary source material from the sixteenth to nineteenth centuries, in her 1983 book *Forgotten Children: Parent-child Relations from 1500 to 1900*, to refute the argument that there was no concept of childhood as a distinct phase of life, and no sensitivity to children's special needs, in Europe before the seventeenth century.

"All pre-modern societies have left little by way of census data . . . or . . . personal memoirs of women, children, servants and slaves."

One result of recent studies has been the realisation that the 'nuclear family' goes back much earlier in history than the Industrial Revolution and that in western societies the household, although sometimes a quite complex entity, has not normally included extended kin. This position holds for ancient Greece and Rome as far as one can see at present.

In classical Athens (fifth-fourth centuries BC), spheres of activity were very different for male and female members of a family and for children and adults. There were frequent occasions, for example, when wives and children did not eat with the men: at symposia at home or at official meals beyond the home male citizens ate together or in company of female non-citizens of the *demi-monde*. Houses built for well-to-do families segregated the women's quarters from the more public areas used by men, thus 'protecting' women (and presumably young children) from the company of all males except kin and very close friends. For poorer families, housing would have been more cramped and women and children would have been forced out of the house to earn a living; their range of extra-familial contacts would thus have been wider. In well-to-do circles, however, women's circumscribed activities and comparative lack of education must have made them less effective educators of their young children than were their Roman counterparts later.

Women in Sparta married older than Athenian women (perhaps around twenty, as opposed to early teens), had greater control over wealth and property, and had greater freedom of activity. Their primary role, however, was the same: to bear legitimate children to their husbands.

The evidence for Greek society in the fifth century BC and the archaic period preceding it is not such as to tell us much about family life. It focusses on public life, especially that of warfare and politics, which leaves room only incidentally for women, children and non-citizens. (Greek drama was highly formalised, and its interpretation for real life remains debatable.) We are further deprived because of the lack of funerary inscriptions for much of the fifth century. Athens' ban on all grave markers except the most simple and unadorned seems to have been provoked by the new democracy's fear of the influence of leading families. Funerals could be the occasion of great family display, as could festivals and anniversaries celebrated at the tomb monument. Even after inscriptions began to reappear, following the outbreak of the Peloponnesian war in 431 BC, they often identified only the dead person and revealed little family history (by contrast with Roman inscriptions which are rich sources for such history).

"Athenian law contained much stronger provisions to keep property within the family than did Roman law later."

Fourth-century literature has preserved many speeches from the law-courts which give an insight into family disputes, especially those to do with inheritance. It was this material particularly which W.K. Lacey (Auckland) exploited in *The Family in Classical Greece*, the first (and still the only) book specifically on this topic. Athenian law contained much stronger provisions to keep property within the family than did Roman law later. Some girls, e.g. orphans with sizeable inheritances, were required to marry a close male relative because females could not inherit fully in their own right. (Spartan females could inherit in their own right.) This requirement could be enforced from the girl's thirteenth birthday.

From the late fourth century on, Greece and the rest of the Eastern Mediterranean were under the control of successive monarchies (the Hellenistic period) and then that of Rome. Roman law applied ever more widely as Roman citizenship spread, but a good deal of autonomy remained for local law and custom, in family as in other matters. By the Roman Imperial period, members of élite families were adopting Roman customs; but the evidence still tells us little about ordinary people in Greek society.

In Roman society of the late Republic and of the Empire the core nuclear family (conjugal couple and dependent children) can be identified at many levels. Its values permeated the whole of society even if death, divorce and celibacy sometimes undermined those values in practice and if slave or non-Roman status made formal attainment of full Roman marriage impossible.

The frequency of divorce and premature death resulted in frequent remarriage. This led to many reconstituted, blended families. Is the model of the simple nuclear family really applicable in such circumstances? The modernity of this is striking: in many contemporary western societies there is no single pattern of 'the family' in practice—divorce occurs often, single-parent and blended families are frequent, there are many childless couples—but the ideal of the enduring conjugal couple co-resident with their own two children remains strong and, in spite of statistics, many (perhaps most) couples enter marriage expecting to follow this pattern. The same picture is recognisable at Rome: the sentimental ideal of family life was strong for a long period of Roman history, as Suzanne Dixon of the University of Queensland has shown.

The legal powers of the *paterfamilias* (the head of household, the oldest surviving male ascendant) were very extensive, and this has sometimes led to a gloomy view of Roman family life, leaving little room for personal autonomy or affection. No doubt discipline was stricter than in many modern western families, and there was a strong conservative thrust in the respect for elders and the emulation of ancestors. The education system reinforced this, with its use of history as models of conduct and its cultivation of national traditions. But severe corporal punishment by fathers was considered humiliating and exceptional treatment for freeborn Roman citizen children (as Saller's recent study of corporal punishment shows); there are various kinds of evidence for the joy which parents took in children; there was considerable scope for dependants to exercise some form of financial and social freedom; women normally remained members of their family of origin and their husband did not become their *paterfamilias*; women could inherit property in their own right; Roman law took care to protect the rights of children; newly married couples established their own households and thus were physically removed from day-to-day intrusion by a *paterfamilias*; and mortality rates ensured that, for many, the *paterfamilias* died at a comparatively early age.

Mortality rates also ensured that parents not infrequently outlived their children. This provoked expressions of grief at many levels of society but it was a special problem for upper-class families, where transmission of name and property was of particular importance. Adoption was sometimes used to achieve such transmission. An adoptee was normally a young adult man. Adoption was not therefore a humanitarian response to the plight of infants or young children at large whose natural parents could not or would not raise them themselves. Most of the emperors of the first two centuries were childless, or their children did not survive to adulthood, so they used adoption to secure an heir. This kind of motivation could hardly have been uppermost in the minds of persons lower down the social scale. Fostering, however, was known and many foster-children must have been orphans or abandoned infants who were saved from almost certain death by being taken up by a foster-parent.

In recent years increasing attention has been devoted to the more modest and lower classes. Many thousands of inscriptions—largely epitaphs—provide precious details which we can increasingly read with understanding: details of age, sex, status, relationship between dedicator and dedicatee, and sometimes of careers and geographical origin.

The very act of setting up funerary inscriptions is not an intrinsic part of human activity, although the desire to leave some record of one's self has been strong in many societies. Not only are such inscriptions very characteristic of Roman society, but the strong family association with such inscriptions is also very Roman. Even in the lower classes, where slave conditions, premature death and economic hardship must have acted against family stability, surviving members (especially parents, children and spouses) came together in surprising numbers to commemorate a member who had died.

Roman nomenclature is a vital clue in studying this evidence. It has helped, for example, identify the status of couples in the city of Rome who lived in a *de facto* marital relationship rather than in a fully legitimated Roman marriage. In most of these relationships, at least one partner had been of slave status when the union began; the partners were thus precluded from full Roman marriage, but their unions could be enduring, often continuing into a period when both had free status and Roman citizenship. (A special category was that of soldiers in the Roman army, who were not allowed to marry until the end of the second century. The law recognised, however, that unions were formed and children produced and early in the second century it made provision for such children—technically illegitimate—to inherit from their fathers if the fathers died during service.) Partners in these relationships often used vocabulary associated with marriage and clearly thought of themselves in many respects as married. Once we realise that it was legal status which made the relationship concubinage or some other type of informal marriage, we understand why terms such as 'concubine' did not attract moral disapproval (although they may have occasioned some social condescension); they were in no way a sign of wilful avoidance of marriage or of promiscuity or of polygamy.

Marriage remained the ideal to which most Romans aspired, but not all were eligible. Those who were ineligible might nevertheless live in a marital-type relationship with one partner for years, and the names of successive children sometimes help chart the improving status of one or both partners: siblings might include slave, ex-slave and freeborn children. It would be hard to think of a more telling indicator of social mobility.

"Marriage remained the ideal to which most Romans aspired, but not all were eligible."

Studies of this kind were developing in Australia (Beryl Rawson, ANU, Canberra) and North America (Susan Treggiari, Ottawa and then Stanford) in the 1960s and 1970s. About the same time Paul Weaver (from the University of Western Australia and then the University of Tasmania) was detailing relationships in a very special *familia*, the Familia Caesaris, i.e. the household of the emperor. This work illuminated the operation of the imperial bureaucracy and showed that imperial slaves and freedmen (ex-slaves) sometimes had such standing, power and wealth (or the potential for these) that women of free—even freeborn—status were prepared to enter marital unions with them. Children of such unions were technically illegitimate and took their status and family name from their mother. 'Illegitimacy' has come to have such pejorative overtones in later western history that it is hardly appropriate in the Roman context, where (like concubinage, mentioned above) it was largely the result of status rather than wilful avoidance of marriage. Evidence of illegitimates in Roman society tends to be found in the legal code (where, by contrast with classical Athenian law, provision could be made for illegitimate children to inherit from their father), in soldiers' records, and in funerary inscriptions. A probable example of such a child is in the modest epitaph (now in the Classics Museum of the Australian National University) set up by M. Gauius Socrates for his mother:

D.M.
M. GAVIVS
SOCRATES GA-
VIAE CHRYSIDI
MATRI B.M.F.

('To the departed spirit of Gauia Chrysis: set up by M. Gauius Socrates for his well-deserving mother').

Although we do not know who was the father (who just might have had the same family name as the mother), it is likely that Gauius Socrates took his name from his mother because his parents' relationship was not a formal Roman marriage.

Epitaph for a mother (first or second century AD), CIL *6.18920 (Classics Department Museum, Australian National University)*

Studies of epitaphs by Saller and Shaw have helped to revise views on the age of marriage of Roman women. Although it remains probable that upper-class women married for the first time in their early teens, other women were more likely to marry in their mid to late teens. It was from about this point that women's epitaphs tended to be dedicated by spouses rather than parents, suggesting that about this age women's primary role was changing from daughter to wife. Men married somewhat later than women, perhaps at an age ten years older, and this had important implications for intra-family relationships and for transmission of property. With the help of the Cambridge Group (mentioned above) Saller has created a possible model of the demographic pattern of the Roman family, showing the probabilities of various relatives surviving other members of the family at different ages. This makes more understandable the workings of *patria potestas* (the power of the *paterfamilias*) and helps confirm the picture of conjugal family (including dependent young children) living in their own household, operating as a discrete social group. Nevertheless, recent study of domestic architecture suggests that 'the big house' was a frequent phenomenon, encompassing kin, other dependants and workers, tenants, lodgers and visitors. We already knew that the term *familia* could include slaves and sometimes ex-slaves, and that the structure of the freestanding Roman house (especially the open-plan *atrium* area) encouraged the attendance of friends, connexions and dependants at particular times of the day or on particular occasions. Andrew Wallace-Hadrill has recently argued that a variety of persons might have had actual co-residence in a big house: as 'housefuls' rather than households, i.e. several independent groups living within one house. This was, of course, the norm for the apartment buildings (*insulae*) which became more popular in the cities of the Imperial period and of which there is such good evidence near Rome at Ostia.

The public-private dichotomy with which we are familiar today was not nearly so clear-cut in ancient Rome. All aspects of life were much more public than we are used to; home and work were not so separated from each other; the domestic physical environment, even for wealthy families, made little provision for private withdrawal; public architecture drew families and individuals out of the home into the street, the forum, the temples, the baths, the theatres and other places of entertainment for festivals and many other public occasions. Women had much greater freedom of movement than had women in classical Greece. Children must have mixed with a wide range of people beyond immediate family, at home and outside, and the socialising effects of this must have been enormous. In Roman society the state took no direct responsibility for education and there were no public institutions for the care of children. Public programs to assist children never envisaged children outside a familial context. There were, however, such programs; and the ideology imposed and fostered by the first emperor, Augustus, and especially his successors in the second century gave the family and children a central place. The imperial regime provided more than two centuries of widespread peace, a time of greater stability, affluence and leisure than ever before for many people. Family relationships probably benefited from this. There was not a sudden or radical change in the system of values, but some development is detectable. More study is necessary to help explain such developments in a society's cultural symbolism and values. Comparative, cross-cultural studies will also contribute to a wider perspective and will enable us to speak with more confidence and understanding about developments in our own society.

References

Further references for the material above may be found in: Beryl Rawson (ed.), *The Family in Ancient Rome: New Perspectives,* London and Ithaca 1986, and *Marriage, Divorce and Children in Ancient Rome*, Oxford 1990. In particular, the 1990 book contains Suzanne Dixon's 'The sentimental ideal of the Roman family', R.P. Saller's 'Corporal punishment, authority and obedience in the Roman household', and Andrew Wallace-Hadrill's 'Houses and households: sampling Pompeii and Herculaneum'. See also:

W.K. Lacey, *The Family in Classical Greece*, London 1968

R.P. Saller, 'Men's age at marriage and its consequences in the Roman family', *Classical Philology* 82 (1987) 21–34

R.P. Saller and B.D. Shaw, 'Tombstones and Roman family relations in the Principate: civilians, soldiers and slaves', *Journal of Roman Studies* 74 (1984) 124–56

B.D. Shaw, 'The age of Roman girls at marriage: some reconsiderations', *Journal of Roman Studies* 77 (1987) 30–46

Susan Treggiari, *Roman Marriage*, Oxford 1991

P.R.C. Weaver, *Familia Caesaris: A Social Study of the Emperor's Freedmen and Slaves*, Cambridge 1972

ATHENS AND JERUSALEM

E.A. Judge
Macquarie University

'What has Athens to do with Jerusalem? Or the Academy with the Church?' These forbidding questions were posed by Tertullian early in the third century. A Roman, from Carthage, he was educated in the same classical tradition we follow. An expert in rhetoric and law, he was also the first major advocate of Christianity writing in Latin. His point was to disqualify heretics from the Church on the charge of compromise with philosophy. 'What have heretics to do with Christians? . . . We have no need of curiosity since Christ Jesus, nor of enquiry since the gospel.'

Judaism was also entrenching itself in the same epoch, though the desecration of Jerusalem and the defeat of the Jewish national hope in the wars of the first and second centuries make that case historically more explicable. The churches moreover had split from the synagogues in favour of emancipation from the law. Paul, too, like other Jewish scholars of the first century, had been used to philosophical argument, though he would not have found it hard to support Tertullian.

The unexpected establishment of Christianity in the fourth century soon turned things around. Chrysostom in the Greek Church and Jerome in the Latin were supreme masters of classical philology, a tradition of learning already a thousand years old. Certainly deep-seated contradictions remained, but now became themselves the object of penetrating study, as one sees above all in Augustine. He is the Aristotle of the West, the most comprehensive and still the most studied of all writers in Classical Latin, preserving for us much that would otherwise have been lost from the ancient world.

Throughout the Middle Ages it was the monasteries that kept and transmitted the texts of classical authors, consolidated into handwritten *codices* (or books). This was the great technological development, fostered by the Christian demand for accessibility of texts (as distinct from the classical and Jewish retention of inconvenient scrolls for literary works), that has literally carried the body of ancient knowledge down to our century.

With the Renaissance and the Reformation of the sixteenth century biblical and classical philology were both revived and pursued within a common discipline. Only in the late eighteenth century did the Enlightenment with its counterfoil, Romanticism, begin to reassert the ideal of a purely classical scholarship. There then developed during the nineteenth and twentieth centuries a separate tradition of biblical criticism and learning. In Germany and Britain this was accommodated within universities in the faculties of Theology, attaining standards of scholarly excellence on a par with those of Classics in the separate faculties of Arts.

In continental Europe the literature of the Church Fathers, rich in citations of the Classics as well as of the Bible, continued to provide a meeting ground of the disciplines. Its scope was vast. The corpus of extant authors in ancient Greek runs to twenty million words for the eight centuries from the sixth BC to the second AD, while the third and fourth (the era of the greatest patristic authors) alone have left another twenty million, and the fifth and sixth (the beginning of the Byzantine era) another twenty. These four last centuries (the third to the sixth) also provided the French and the Germans in particular with the sources of their national history; it was the classical scholars who edited such texts for their historical colleagues.

In Britain, however, the classicists typically ended their curriculum early in the second century. The great Cambridge Histories fixed the end of Ancient History and the beginning of Mediaeval at Constantine. Now the new Cambridge Ancient History is set to retrieve some of the later centuries for antiquity. More particularly, we are now seeing the fairly rapid development of a new sub-field of study amongst English-language classical scholars. It is called 'Late Antiquity'. It embraces the third to the sixth centuries inclusive.

The fact that books now often take this term to define their scope, whereas no journal has yet been created to serve it, points to its transitional status. The watershed was crossed by the late A.H.M. Jones, Professor of Ancient History at Cambridge. He demonstrated in the 'sixties how the reservoir of patristic sources might be tapped for historical research on secular themes. Ancient historians at Oxford began to produce biographical and cultural studies of leading figures of Late Antiquity who had previously been the preserve of theologians. Notable here was Peter Brown's work on Augustine.

Antichthon was founded as 'a journal of ancient world studies' embracing not only Greece and Rome, but 'the Ancient Near East and the Mediterranean from the beginning of civilisation to the Early Middle Ages'. It publishes articles relating to 'the languages, literature, history, thought and archaeology of the ancient world'. This broad scope was adopted to allow, amongst other things, the inclusion of biblical alongside classical studies. So far as the journal goes, this has barely happened. Journals have a life of their own, and people prefer to publish where they will be read by their own kind. *Antichthon* has grown up to become no more than a regular Classics journal.

But the last two decades have nevertheless seen a strong growth of academic work in Australia that spans the biblical/classical divide. In what follows I mention only work done within the universities, and mainly therefore under the disciplines of Ancient History or Classics, omitting a great deal of professional publication in biblical and patristic studies done within the theological colleges. I group my comments under the three rubrics of (a) language, (b) history, and (c) thought.

(a) ***'The songs of Zion . . . in a strange land' (Psalm 137.3–4)***
The partnership of biblical and classical philology in Early Modern times was not an unqualified bonus. It permitted at least two basic misconceptions which have been criticised especially by Australian researchers in the past two decades.

Biblical Hebrew was analysed in the West by scholars for whom Latin was the *lingua franca*, and its rules, derived from Classical Greek grammar, were applied also to the definition of Hebrew. But while Greek and Latin are Indo-European languages, Hebrew is a Semitic one. There is no close family relationship (although it was a Semitic alphabet that established itself in the Mediterranean, presumably through early Greek trading contact with the Levant).

Modern linguistic science has developed principles of analysis that can be applied to any language (the impetus for this often coming from the vast modern enterprise of Bible translation). The computerisation of languages has in turn supplied a mode of analysing them uncontaminated by any preconception as to their structure. Using this double advantage offered to our generation, Francis I. Andersen developed an altogether fresh syntax of biblical Hebrew. His work both is massively challenging and has provoked criticism. But the emancipation of Hebrew from Greek will be a lasting gain.

Biblical Greek, on the other hand, was often read in Early Modern times in the light of Hebrew. In particular the peculiarities of the ancient Septuagint translation of the Hebrew Bible into Greek, and of the New Testament, have been explained as 'Jewish Greek'. This goes beyond the phenomenon of Semitisms in the New Testament, carefully analysed by Max Wilcox.

There is no doubt that, by classical standards, there are oddities to be explained. When the great papyrus discoveries began in Egypt at the end of the last century, Deissmann and Moulton were quick to observe the affinities between the Greek of the New Testament and that of the private letters and business documents of its times. Their work was influential, but in the field of semantics it was overrun by the biblical theology movement of the 'thirties. Fuelled by the opposition to Hitler, New Testament studies affirmed its Hebraic sources.

But the analysis of the Greek language of those times proceeded with reference to the *koine* ('common') Greek. At Sydney the late George Shipp practised this historical treatment of the language. *Antichthon* opened with a sample of his work, and others were published over the years. Work on the *koine* was maintained by John Lee. His lexical study of the Septuagint demonstrated that many of its peculiarities need not be explained as 'Jewish'. They are attested in the ordinary papyrus documents of Ptolemaic times.

Enoch Powell, in his inaugural lecture as Professor of Greek at Sydney in 1938, finished with the claim that, 'with the possible exception of papyrology, there is no branch of classical research which either now or at any conceivable future time can be carried on effectively at Sydney'. Microfilm and air travel have long since altered the scene. But his one positive prophecy has in fact been fulfilled. At Macquarie in the 'seventies, a start was made with the study of unpublished papyri. Stuart Pickering, curator of the growing collection, soon spotted a third-century fragment of the Acts of the Apostles.

We were urged to update Moulton and Milligan's fifty-year-old classic on the vocabulary of the New Testament, based upon the first wave of publication of documentary papyri. Greg Horsley then produced a five-volume series, bringing more recently published texts, including many inscriptions from the Eastern Mediterranean, to bear on the question of New Testament Greek. With the aid of recent linguistic work on how languages interact in a bilingual community, he has decisively fortified the conclusions of Deissmann and Moulton, and also refined the conventional polarisation between 'atticising' and *koine* Greek with reference to the concept of linguistic 'register'. So far as the New Testament goes, we cannot speak of 'Jewish', let alone 'Christian', Greek, as though there were a separate dialect being formed.

The Latin language as used by the Church Fathers has also provided a key to cultural history. Deeply influenced as the Fathers were by the 'Old Latin' version of the Bible, as well as by the specialised vocabulary of church life, their writings must be understood both in relation to the ongoing norms of Ciceronian latinity, and to the way they reflect the life of the times. The strength of such an understanding has been richly demonstrated by Graeme Clarke in his five volumes of detailed commentary on the work of two North African compatriots of and fellow-believers with Tertullian, the 'Octavius' of Minucius Felix and the letters of Cyprian. They reveal the complex interrelation of classical and Christian traditions during the cataclysms of the third century.

In Egypt a flourishing Jewish community was largely obliterated in the revolt of AD 114–117. The documentary traces of Christianity do not begin until after that. In the third century, the ancient language of Egypt, long submerged for administrative purposes by Greek, reappeared in a popular form with a simplified script based on the Greek alphabet. It was the product of the Christian principle of translating Scripture into the vernacular. Thus Coptic ('Egyptian') emerged to survive into our own time as the language of the Egyptian Church. Geoff Jenkins studies the Coptic translations of the Bible, and works on the important Greek and Coptic papyri already found by the Melbourne expedition to the Dakleh Oasis, where a christianised settlement of the third to the fifth centuries was abandoned until our own day. Michael Lattke is producing a five-volume treatment of the Odes of Solomon, early Christian hymns translated from Greek into Syriac and Coptic. With Syriac similarly the churches have preserved the Aramaic of Jesus' time as an ecclesiastical language, much studied in the past generation at both Melbourne and Sydney Universities.

(b) ***'Not many mighty . . . are called' (1 Corinthians 1.26)***
Language is an important index of social level. Deissmann drew an emphatic conclusion from his discovery that the New Testament was written in the 'common' Greek. The apostles then were common men, and it was as men of the people that they took over the ancient world. According to Arnold Toynbee, they were a classic 'internal proletariat', subverting the old civilisation from within. But the 'common' Greek was not spoken only by common people. It was the standard Greek of the professional and technical writers of its century. The half illiterate letters on papyrus are only a vulgar form of it. The Pauline communities especially were plainly dominated by highly articulate people with social pretensions. Paul put them down ('not many mighty') to make a point of principle. The Pauline churches created a novel set of social relations, linking people of different status.

Robert Banks produced an eloquent semi-popular presentation of these social arrangements. The evidence is so direct that its interpretation is tricky. The Oxford ancient historian Geoffrey de Ste Croix, writing as a Marxist, held that Paul wrote a blank cheque for the powers that be and sold out the proletarian initiative of Jesus. My own view is that Paul rather severed the bond between rank and status, endorsing any formally recognised responsibility within the existing social order but stripping it of social privilege: in his terms, converting leadership into service. It was more than his status-hungry promoters could tolerate. Peter Marshall explains the resultant imbroglio in terms of the classic ritual of enmity, which he defined from the contemporary sources and for the first time applied to New Testament interpretation.

The first known attempt to set the experiences of the churches and the Pauline mission in an historical perspective, and relate them to the gospel of Jesus, is preserved in the Gospel of Luke and the

Acts of the Apostles, a double work of the one author. The late Robert Maddox and Philip Esler have both treated the interpretative problems that arise, one in the more classic discipline, the other by a sociological approach. Historians of ancient Judaism contribute to the debate. The Jewish matrix of Jesus is explored by Max Wilcox. Paul Barnett, whose specialty is the Jewish revolutionary movements of the first century, writes of the 'new quest' for the historical Jesus. This does not so much distance the gospels from historical contact with him (as the older 'quest' did), as use them to pin him down as an historically recognisable Jewish type. Alan Crown has specialised in the history of the Samaritans and other Jewish sects which formed a continuing link between Judaism and the churches in patristic times.

The Jews were a recognised nation, entitled to keep their ancient customs and having therefore a history, even though their state was lost. The Christians, however, had set themselves up in no-man's-land. They impudently claimed the Jewish patriarchs as validating their own position—in a backward-looking epoch one strove to capture the authority of antiquity. Though mostly Greeks and Romans by birth they neglected their social obligation, and made up customs for themselves. They and their opponents actually agreed on the interpretation of this: they were acting as if they too were a nation.

The enterprise of Luke/Acts was picked up by Eusebius early in the fourth century. Yet the conversion of Constantine distracted him from understanding that state within the state that the churches have since demonstrated themselves to be. By the creation of a fundamental right to self-determination these paradoxical arrangements have become one of the foundations of Western political and social culture.

The study of how it came to be historically sensed is approached in the treatment of the theme of recurrence by Gary Trompf and in two symposia, edited by Brian Croke and Alanna Emmett and then by Graeme Clarke with the support of his two predecessors and Raoul Mortley. The ancient writers, whether classical or Christian, all failed to create an historical treatment that could cope with the incommensurability of the now parallel and rival traditions. We too have still to master this dilemma.

(c) ***'Philosophy and vain deceit' (Colossians 2.8)***

Tertullian glosses Athens and Jerusalem as the Academy and the Church, not the Parthenon and the Church. The dispute is not essentially about the cult or worship of God. It is an intellectual dispute about the true understanding of the world and of man's place in it. Philosophy is repudiated precisely because it is philosophy that occupies the high ground the Church will capture.

'Religion', in the common Roman sense of cultic practice, has little if anything to do with the issue. Many philosophers were just as critical of the intellectual contradictions of cult and myth as the churches were—indeed the latter happily took over the philosophical critique of them. The classical cults in general prescribed neither belief nor behaviour. The fact that we now mean by 'religion' a system of behaviour based on beliefs is a measure of the success of the fourth-century churches in taking on the popular trappings of the old cults. Thus a basic shift of great historical moment was brought to pass in the ordering of public life. In classical times the cult of the gods was almost invariably devoted to safeguarding the status quo. Whether national or personal, the rituals anchored one in a unified order. The new monopoly of the churches detached 'religion' from the State.

The fact that Caesar was a Christian did not alter this. Constantine quickly made clear that he submitted to the judgement of the bishops. Ambrose, Bishop of Milan, successfully demanded penance of Theodosius for a political atrocity. At the same time the cultic power of the churches over the masses gave them their triumph over philosophy in the social arena. It was not that the churches lost their commitment to doctrine. Far from it. Rather they mobilised much of the community to doctrinal causes and drastically reshaped the social order into the bargain. (I have in mind the stunning impact on the fourth-century mind of such social innovations as synodical debates, charity for the poor, and the attempted repudiation of social life altogether in monasticism.)

Philosophy was outclassed. The philosophers for their part could mount a telling critique of the churches in social terms, and in both Stoicism and Platonism they had long developed their own intellectual modus vivendi with religion. But their social impotence was displayed for the whole world to see when Julian attempted to convert the ancient cults into Church-like action-groups in the name of philosophical Hellenism. No one even took him seriously. Yet in his tragic way the young heir of the house of Constantine, brought up by bishops but a secret renegade to the old cults, saw more clearly than anyone on either side the historic consequences of what was happening before their eyes.

The unity of the classical culture of a thousand years was destroyed forever, and this had been achieved by the promotion of a rival kind of education. This gave Julian one other weapon against them. Since they did not believe in the gods, let the Christians not teach classical literature either. Let them educate their own young from the Bible, since they believed in that. But the last thing the churches wanted was Christian schools. The Bible could not provide an education in Classical Greek. So it was hastily recast into the appropriate literary forms, a paradox saved from itself by the premature death of Julian.

The competition with the philosophers, however, was not about literature nor even about methods of argument. The intellectual discipline was shared. It was not a matter of blind faith pitted against relentless reason. Both sides held tenaciously to a dogmatic tradition, yet one hotly contested in either case amongst its own adherents. The differences lay in their basic understanding of the world. On the one side a single cosmic order, self-contained, stable and eternal, embracing gods and men alike, each in his limited sphere. On the other, a world made by God, with man the centre of attention, vital decisions to be made and events to come.

The ideals of behaviour were correspondingly at odds. The philosophical tradition sought individual development within social harmony, with the aim of preserving the integrity of the soul against the accidents of the body. The churches focussed on the consciousness of evil within man, and sought the solution within the sphere of physical life in the community, a life of commitment and compassion. Plotinus dismissed the suffering of the weak as a just reward for their misdeeds. Augustine, as one of the newly discovered letters reveals, forcibly rescued the victims of the press-gangs, and brought political influence to bear on the government to soften the law so that it could effectively be applied to the high-status perpetrators.

In sharpening these antitheses I make no attempt to relate my observations to the notable series of works on the interaction of the philosophical and Christian traditions produced by Eric Osborn and Raoul Mortley. I am well aware of the intricate ways in which the two traditions intersect. I am also well aware that the reigning position amongst ancient historians, both ancient and ecclesiastical, is that precious little changed in terms of actual behaviour. Indeed the life of many became more brutal in the christianised Late Antiquity. And certainly the new order drained away the civic spirit that had sustained classical culture.

Yet the Classics remain, and their legacy is deeply imprinted on our own moral culture. The same goes for the Bible. The contradictions between them are built into everyone's make-up now, whatever an individual's particular commitments or behaviour. The rivalry within the soul of man, and the public confrontation of Church and State, both contribute decisively to the distinctive freedom and quality of life in the West. From an educational point of view the two traditions surely belong together.

Bibliographical Note

Works by Australian scholars of the past generation are here listed in the order they are referred to in the discussion above.

(a) Francis I. Andersen, *The Hebrew Verbless Clause in the Pentateuch*, Nashville

1970; *The Sentence in Biblical Hebrew*, The Hague 1974; Max Wilcox, 'Semitisms in the New Testament', *Aufstieg und Niedergang der römischen Welt* 2.25.2, Berlin 1984; G.P. Shipp, *Modern Greek Evidence for the Ancient Greek Vocabulary*, Sydney 1979; J.A.L. Lee, *A Lexical Study of the Septuagint Version of the Pentateuch*, Chico 1983; G.H.R. Horsley, *New Documents Illustrating Early Christianity*, 5 vols, Sydney 1981–1989; Graeme W. Clarke, *The Octavius of Minucius Felix*, New York 1974; *The Letters of St Cyprian of Carthage*, 4 vols, New York 1984–1989; Michael Lattke, *Die Oden Salomos in ihrer Bedeutung für Neues Testament und Gnosis*, 5 vols, Göttingen 1979 ff.

(b) R.J. Banks, *Paul's Idea of Community: The Early House-Churches in their Historical Setting*, Sydney 1979; E.A. Judge, *Rank and Status in the World of the Caesars and St. Paul*, Christchurch 1982; Peter J. Marshall, *Enmity at Corinth: Social Conventions in Paul's Relations with the Corinthians*, Tübingen 1987; R.J. Maddox, *The Purpose of Luke–Acts*, Edinburgh 1982; P.F. Esler, *Community and Gospel in Luke-Acts: The Social and Political Motivations of Lucan Theology*, Cambridge 1987; Max Wilcox, 'Jesus in the light of his Jewish environment', *Aufstieg und Niedergang der römischen Welt* 2.25.1, Berlin 1982; Paul W. Barnett, *The Two Faces of Jesus*, Sydney 1990; A.D. Crown (ed.), *Samaritans*, Tübingen 1989; G.W. Trompf, *The Idea of Historical Recurrence in Western Thought from Antiquity to the Reformation*, Berkeley 1979; B.F. Croke and Alanna M. Emmett (eds), *History and Historians in Late Antiquity*, Sydney 1983; G.W. Clarke, with B.F. Croke, R.J. Mortley and Alanna Emmett-Nobbs, *Reading the Past in Late Antiquity*, Canberra 1990.

(c) E.F. Osborn, *Justin Martyr*, Tübingen 1973; *Ethical Patterns in Early Christian Thought*, Cambridge 1976; *The Beginning of Christian Philosophy*, Cambridge 1981; R.J. Mortley, *Connaissance religieuse et herméneutique chez Clément d'Alexandrie*, Leiden 1973; 'Gnosis', *Reallexikon für Antike und Christentum*, Münster 1980; *From Word to Silence: I The Rise and Fall of Logos, II The Way of Negation, Christian and Greek*, Bonn 1986; *Désir et différence dans la tradition platonicienne*, Paris 1988.

SIXTH-CENTURY BYZANTIUM AND THE END OF CLASSICAL ANTIQUITY

Roger Scott
University of Melbourne

Helena, discoverer of the True Cross and indeed one of the most successful archaeologists in the Holy Land of all time, was honoured by her son Constantine, the first Christian emperor, by the renaming of the village of Drepanon in Bithynia as Helenoupolis (now the Turkish village of Hersek), so giving it city status. Constantine, however, had not done the job properly, as the sixth-century historian Prokopios tells us in book 5 of his *Buildings*, so it was left to Prokopios' own emperor Justinian to make Helenoupolis into a real city. Justinian,

> as though to compensate for this failing by the empire's forefather, seeing first that the city was in difficulty from its lack of water and was usually suffering from a terrible thirst, improvised a magnificent <aqueduct> by which sufficient water, an unexpected sight, was provided not only for drinking by the population there but also for bathing and the other luxuries of those who have an abundant supply of it. In addition he built a public bath for them, which had not existed before, and he restored another one, which lay broken and abandoned because of the shortage of water, as has been stated, and had already collapsed from neglect. He also built here churches, a palace, stoas and lodgings for officials, and for the rest he made the prosperity of the city obvious.

Nearby in other parts of Bithynia as well as elsewhere in his empire, Justinian built city-walls and bridges, diverted rivers (to avoid flood damage) and above all constructed roads. Near Antioch in Syria, for instance, there was a dangerously narrow track through the mountains. Again Prokopios tells us that Justinian,

> paying out an inordinate sum of money, cut through all the mountains which rise there for a great distance, overcoming the impossible; and contrary to all expectations he created a carriageway, making flat and open what had previously been precipitous.

The classicist will recognise here the survival into the sixth century of at least something of the ideal of the Roman city with its standard amenities: baths well-supplied by an aqueduct, the grid-plan open layout with an agora or forum, gymnasia, theatres, hippodrome or amphitheatre, city-walls and good roads both within the city and outside linking it to neighbouring cities and villages. The similarity of these cities right across the Roman empire was such that travellers from Roman Gaul or Spain would have been able to find their way round a Roman city in North Africa or Syria and still enjoy the same amenities

"The classicist will recognise . . . the survival into the sixth century of at least something of the ideal of the Roman city with its standard amenities . . ."

as in their home city. This was still true in the sixth century. Opposite Constantinople lay Galata, then called Sycae, where in 528/9 Justinian restored the theatre and the walls and also built a bridge at the head of the Golden Horn linking Galata to Constantinople. Much further east, at Mocesus in Cappadocia, Justinian built a strong wall and 'there too he built many churches, hospices, public baths and everything else that marks out a prosperous city'. In the other direction, in Libya at Caputvada (now Ras Kaboudia), Justinian

> immediately wanted to transform the place into a city, strengthened by a wall and noted as a proud and prosperous city for its other amenities. The emperor's aim has been achieved. For with a wall completed there is a city, and what was rural is suddenly changed. Countryfolk, having tossed their ploughs aside, now live like a city community, following a lifestyle that is not rustic but urbane. They spend their days in the market-place, hold meetings on the issues which concern them, trade with one another and do all the other things which depend on city status (*Buildings*, 6).

This last example not only shows that the ideal of city life was present in sixth-century Libya but also emphasises one aspect of that ideal, that life should be lived out of the domestic house, whether in assemblies and market places, as here, or at the baths, which are stressed in Prokopios' other examples, or in the formal places of entertainment such as the theatre (e.g. at Galata) or in the hippodrome at Constantinople (wild-beast shows in the amphitheatre had been banned at the end of the fifth century by the emperor Anastasios). Such outdoor life was very much part of the tradition of the classical Roman city. It is also a feature which separates the classical world most clearly from the medieval. Despite much progress in recent years which has made the label of 'the Dark Ages' less easy to apply, information about the seventh and eighth centuries is still difficult to ascertain with any confidence. But when information starts to become available again in the ninth century we are in a changed world.

Instead of cities arranged on a grid plan and standing in an open plain, we now find villages, or rather hill-top forts, with winding lanes that led to the main building which was the church. Instead of the inhabitants, who were in any case much diminished in number, leaving their houses to spend their day in the agora, or more especially at the baths, or attending some other form of entertainment in the theatre, amphitheatre or hippodrome, they now stayed indoors as much as possible, venturing forth to attend church or to take part in state ceremonial, which was itself increasingly religious in character. Even

"Byzantine man . . . felt no great attachment . . . to his community in the way which was so characteristic of the society of Greek and Roman antiquity."

church was avoided as too public a place by those who could afford to pay for their own chapels and retain a household priest, as Cyril Mango has pointed out. Distrust rather than a common bond characterised community relations. For instance the eleventh-century Cecaumenos tells us:

> Never put up a friend in your house, since the friend may seduce your wife. Let him lodge elsewhere and send him the necessary food. Lock up your daughters as if they were criminals. Avoid all parties. If you are not on the emperor's business, stay at home with your trusted servants, stockpile supplies and look after the interests of your family. (Mango 1980, 82).

Byzantine man, certainly as typified by Cecaumenos, now clearly felt no great attachment to his *polis* or to his community in the way which was so characteristic of the society of Greek and Roman antiquity. This is of course a wildly general claim, and distinctions based on area, time and indeed the individual need to be made and are being made in recent scholarship. Thus for seventh-century Byzantine Italy, a recent study by T.S. Brown (formerly of ANU) can show how army officers were able to exploit insecurity and the decline of civil institutions by insinuating themselves into an urban and agrarian network which remained largely intact. That is, Italy both shared and differed from the characteristics that I have mentioned. But whatever variations a more detailed study would cover, the characteristics of classical society, especially the amenities of the city and the feeling of being part of a community, had largely disappeared.

By contrast these characteristics were very much present in the sixth century, and one can widen them to include aspects of literature and art, where classical imitation is evident. For instance the student of classical literature will have a feeling of *déjà vu* with the following passage:

> Prokopios of Caesarea has written the history of the wars which

> Justinian, the Roman emperor, waged against the barbarians of the east and of the west, just as each happened, so that the great length of time may not overwhelm outstanding deeds through lack of a record, consign them to oblivion and render them quite extinct. The recollection of these deeds he thought would be a great thing and especially useful to both present and future generations, if ever again time should place men in a similar crisis.

Prokopios continues in his preface to imitate not only Thucydides and Herodotus but also Diodorus Siculus and parades further imitations of such well known episodes in Thucydides as the plague and the siege of Plataea. Much the same can be said of Agathias' history a little later in the century, though more interesting is the collection made by Agathias of short poems written by various contemporaries, again all in classical metres, imitating classical themes and restricted as far as possible to classical language. Despite the artificiality of this (and it did require artificiality; the distinctions between long and short vowels, which were the basis of the classical metres, had long disappeared from the spoken language as had much of the vocabulary being used), the poets were conscious that they were really doing something new and this remains an especial strength of much of their poetry, which deserves a new, more sympathetic study. We have here some of the strengths of a genuine classical tradition, i.e. material that certainly would not have come into being but for classical models, but which is itself new, conscious of its novelty and full of life and quality. But again it is difficult, if not impossible, to find work of such quality (especially where it owes a debt to the classical tradition) after the sixth century until the tenth century at the earliest.

What, however, is just as revealing in classical imitation is the evidence of change. Agathias' poets wrote several pieces about civil servants. Prokopios adapted Thucydides to suit contemporary situations. For instance, despite Prokopios' classicism, he cannot really cope with Thucydides' rationalism. Prokopios' account of plague occurs in a world where all could be explained and solved in terms of monotheism and monarchy. Averil Cameron in a recent study has also shown that it is Prokopios' classicism that really separates him from his age, and that for all his imitation of the language of his classical models, when it comes to the interpretation of events, Prokopios is extremely superficial and limited.

If we turn to the works of his contemporaries, the classical world recedes very rapidly. The chronicle of John Malalas provides a history of the world from Creation to the end of the reign of Justinian. In it Classical Greece hardly gets a mention. There are just occasional lists of great names. For instance, under Philip of Macedon, Malalas claims that 'the philosophers and poets Sophokles, Herakleitos,

Euripides, Herodotos, Sokrates and the great Pythagoras were the teachers of Hellenic learning'. Admittedly the Olympian gods are present by name, but in Malalas they are not gods but emperors and they have no connexion with Greece, Kronos being emperor of Italy, Zeus of Persia and later Italy, while Helios succeeds his father Hephaistos as ruler of Egypt. The Roman Republic is similarly ignored. Contemporary hymns help emphasise this rejection of the classical world. The *Akathistos* hymn, which was written in either the fifth or sixth century, includes the following lines in its praise of the Virgin:

> Hail, to you who show the philosophers to be fools;
> hail to you who prove men of letters to be men of no wisdom;
> hail to you, for able disputers have been shown to be idiots;
> hail to you, for the fashioners of fables have been made to wither;
> hail to you who have torn apart the intricate schemes of the Athenians.
> (trans. C. Trypanis, *Penguin Book of Greek Verse*, 384–5).

And Romanos, the greatest of Byzantium's hymn-writers, is equally hostile to the classics:

> Why do the Greeks snort and chatter?
> Why do they make a show of Aratus, the thrice-accursed?
> Why are they led into error by Plato?
> Why do they love Demosthenes, the weak?
> Why do they not see that Homer is a flitting dream?
> Why do they keep talking about Pythagoras who justly is to be muzzled?
> (trans. M. Carpenter, *Kontakia of Romanos*, I.367).

Yet, despite this, Romanos still shows signs that he too had benefited from some kind of a classical training in rhetoric, as does a sixth-century flat-earther, Cosmas Indicopleustes, who in his *Christian Topography* argued that the universe was modelled on the Tabernacle.

The presence of the classical world in the sixth century is thus somewhat ambivalent. Certainly the amenities of the classical city were still there both in fact and as an ideal, and certainly the better educated were still reading and imitating classical literature. But they were also clearly living in a world which was in many respects very different from the classical world, which could be seen as either irrelevant or hostile. To those trained in classical literature it is only too easy to equate 'difference from the classical world' with 'decline from the classical world' and see even sixth-century classicism as a pale imitation of the real thing. But to do this ignores the achievement of the sixth century and the excitement of its people in their achievement, which we can still share.

If we just limit ourselves to the first decade of Justinian's rule, we have the building of Hagia Sophia, erected in a remarkable six years and unquestionably the orthodox church's greatest building; the reconquest of Africa (Libya) from the Vandals and Italy from the Goths; the signing of the eternal peace with Persia and above all the codification of Roman law, a mammoth achievement requiring a remarkable degree of energy and organisation whether in collecting books and material, selecting suitable staff and distributing them in appropriate committees with the least interference to their normal activities, developing an

"The survival and arguably the creation of Rome's greatest gift is the work of a handful of people between 528 and 534."

excerpting and card-filing system and establishing (and maintaining) a timetable for the completion of the work. The codification is particularly worth reflecting on, given that it is a truism that law was Rome's greatest gift to civilisation. Two points: first, Roman law was in an awful mess by the sixth century and had been so for a long time; second, the survival and arguably the creation of Rome's greatest gift is the work of a handful of people between 528 and 534.

The codification of the law can be seen easily enough in terms of our classical heritage. The hymns of Romanos, on the other hand, cannot, but they provide writing that is exciting by any standard with their use of narrative, dialogue, visual imagery and characterisation, though they remain virtually unknown to most students of ancient Greek. It would be out of place to enter into any discussion of them here. The point, however, is that for at least part of the sixth century not only were there important achievements taking place but some of these great achievements are outside the classical tradition. The notion of a 'decline from classical standards' is just not appropriate. The sixth century, especially the first half, has so much to offer even if phrases like a 'Golden Age' are no longer acceptable. But it is also a world in which some of the features which supposedly distinguish post-Dark-Age Byzantium are already present. The growth of imperial and religious ceremonial, the importance of Christian symbolism in the propaganda of the emperor, the increasing importance of the cult of the Virgin and the incorporation of her cult within official ceremonial—these are all evident by the sixth century or earlier. I have already pointed to the rejection of classical culture in the hymns of Romanos and in the Christian topography of Cosmas Indicopleustes, the downgrading of Ancient Greece and Republican Rome in Malalas' world history, while even in Prokopios' lists of the essential features of a city churches always figure prominently. Fear and suspicion of neighbours is documented clearly enough in Prokopios' *Secret History*, and is hinted at in John Lydus' *On Signs* and in Malalas, while the influence of Holy Men helps separate the sixth century from the classical world and place it firmly in the medieval. St. Daniel for instance, who lived for 33 years on top of a column outside Constantinople, was consulted on foreign policy by the emperor Leo, disastrously as it happens, but his influence was unabated and maintained in the reign of Leo's successor Zeno. To attempt to explain the difference between the sixth century and the period after the Dark Age is well beyond the scope of this paper, but it does need emphasising that, despite the survival of some aspects of the classical world, the sixth century was already showing some of the characteristics of medieval Byzantium.

This leads to a final point. What characterises the classical world perhaps even more than city life is the importance of rhetoric. Rhetoric certainly is still important in late Byzantium, but it is a revival (from the tenth century) rather than a survival. Ann Moffatt has pointed to the decline in the teachers of rhetoric in the sixth century and their virtual disappearance in the seventh. The dominance that rhetoric had maintained in the syllabus was largely due to the practical skills it gave its students and consequently the opportunities it opened for them, even though its exponents would have placed as much emphasis on the moral qualities they claimed it inculcated. But doubts about that relevance are already present in the fourth century, where different practical skills, such as shorthand-writing and accountancy, were being seen as having greater relevance and certainly offering their practitioners more opportunity for rapid advancement. That trend is certainly fostered in the fifth century with the emphasis on practical skills in the so-called Theodosian University in Constantinople. How much can be made of Justinian's closing of the Platonic Academy in Athens in 529 remains a moot point. What is clear is that Justinian persecuted intellectuals, seemingly on charges of paganism. Connected with this, though difficult to document, is yet further emphasis on the new technical skills and the abandoning of the old. Those trained in classical rhetoric may still get jobs at court as minor functionaries and be used to prepare suitable propaganda. Among these were several of the better poets of Agathias' *Cycle* whose interest lay more in literature than in exploiting their technical skills as lawyers. But the reason given for the creation of a new law syllabus by Justinian in 534 *(The Institutes)* was to provide the state apparatus with technically trained lawyers rather than the old-fashioned lawyers whose training in rhetoric may have made them more cultured but who were no longer seen as offering much practical benefit to the state. The same emphasis on a practical education can probably be discerned in other areas as well. John Lydus complains of uneducated new recruits to the civil service who can just fill in forms. The result does appear to have been the abandonment of rhetoric as the staple of education, which it had been for the previous millennium. It is difficult to avoid seeing this as not only helping to bring about the paucity of writers in the seventh and eighth centuries, but actually being identical with it. To that extent a government-sponsored emphasis on practical education brought about the Dark Ages.

Further Reading

Procopius, *History of the Wars; Secret History; Buildings,* trans. H.B. Dewing, 7 vols, Cambridge, Mass. 1914–40

T.S. Brown, *Gentlemen and Officers: Imperial Administration and Aristocratic Power in Byzantine Italy, AD 554–800*, London 1984

A.M. Cameron, *Continuity and Change in Sixth-Century Byzantium*, London 1981

——*Procopius and the Sixth Century*, London 1985

G.W. Clarke (ed.), *Reading the Past in Late Antiquity*, Canberra 1990

A. Honoré, *Tribonian*, London 1978

E.M. Jeffreys, M.J. Jeffreys and R.D. Scott, *The Chronicle of John Malalas: A Translation*, Melbourne 1986

E.M. Jeffreys with B. Croke and R.D. Scott (eds), *Studies in John Malalas*, Sydney 1990

C. Mango, *Byzantium, the Empire of New Rome*, London 1980

——*Byzantium and its Image*, London 1984

M.A. Moffatt, 'Science teachers in the early Byzantine empire', *Byzantinoslavica* 34 (1973) 15–18

M.E. Mullett and R.D. Scott (eds), *Byzantium and the Classical Tradition*, Birmingham 1981

CLASSICAL STUDIES IN AUSTRALIA: SOME IMPRESSIONS

Greg Stanton
University of New England

When classicists explain to people to whom they are introduced what they do for a living—teaching Latin and Greek, as well as Ancient History or Classical Literature by means of texts in translation—the response often suggests that there must be hardly any students. But that is not the case. As with the traditional modern languages taught in Australia, numbers of students in Greek and Latin hit the bottom of the curve a decade or more ago. There has been a steady rise in student numbers since then. In the universities classes for beginners in Latin and Greek are larger, often much larger, than those for students who have matriculated in the language. Beginners' classes in Latin have sixty students in them in at least two universities (Melbourne and Queensland). My own university has fifty students studying Greek and seventy studying Latin at various levels, including six taking Honours in one or both languages. Of course, units which require no knowledge of the ancient languages are far more popular. First-year classes with more than 200 students are not unusual.

There are now thirteen universities teaching ancient world studies in Australia and five in New Zealand. In addition to the large universities (Queensland, Sydney, Macquarie, Melbourne, Monash, Adelaide and Western Australia) in each mainland Australian state, there are Classics departments at the universities of Tasmania, New England and Newcastle and at the Australian National University in Canberra. La Trobe has a Classics presence in several departments, as well as in the Office of the Vice-Chancellor. The Dean of Humanities and Social Sciences (currently Acting Vice-Chancellor) at Bond University is a classicist who is introducing courses on Greek democracy and on the origins of the Christian culture. Five of the departments teaching Classical studies have ten or more academic staff. The University of Melbourne has brought together classicists, archaeologists, Semitic and Modern Greek scholars into a Department of Classical and Near Eastern Studies numbering twenty staff. At the University of Sydney ancient world interests have hitherto been catered for by separate departments of Latin, Greek and Archaeology, and the Ancient History section of History, but these are now being amalgamated into a single school with approximately twenty staff. In addition, there are staff with ancient world interests in the departments of Religious Studies and Semitic Studies.

Research is an important part of the work of universities, even if heavier teaching loads have made it increasingly difficult for academic staff to find adequate time for it. With the aid of Inter-Library Loan, serious research into the ancient world can be and is carried out in Australia. In 1988–89 alone scholars in Australia published books on Egyptian, Greek and Italian archaeology, Athenian democracy, Athenian officials, women in Athens, Alexander the Great, Virgil, Juvenal, women in Rome, Roman law and politics, Roman coins, early Christian and Byzantine writers, and the Classical heritage. Several journals—*Antichthon, Mediterranean Archaeology, Ramus* and (formerly) *Apeiron*—are or have been published in Australia. Large-scale funding is rare in the humanities (except for archaeological projects, on which Graeme Clarke reports in this volume), but research personnel have been funded in recent years for a wide range of projects, including Greek history and inscriptions, Greek warfare and society, women and the family in Rome, the administration of the Roman empire,

"One of the advantages of the ancient world . . . is that it offers the detachment of distance in time and place."

the vocabulary of the Greek New Testament, early Christianity, papyrus documents from Egypt, the linguistic structure of Hebrew, rock-cut Semitic inscriptions, Byzantine historians, Mediaeval Greek literature and Renaissance literature in Latin. One of the advantages of the ancient world as an area of study is that it offers the detachment of distance in time and place. We can be more objective in our investigations. If we can study the effects of warfare on Greek society, or the relationship between Roman mothers and their children, we can surely bring to bear on problems in our own civilisation a different perspective and greater understanding of the human condition.

In the secondary schools, student numbers in Latin have started to rise after a severe decline in the 60s and 70s. The language has been introduced or re-introduced in many schools, though there is as yet no sign of the boom in the study of Latin being experienced, especially in inner-city schools, in the United States. Greek is still taught to matriculation standard in most but not all Australian states. However, non-language courses suitable for the broad range of students now staying at school for Years 11 and 12 have proved popular. In Victoria, for example, Classical Civilisation (now 'Classical Societies and Cultures') has maintained its student numbers, following a marked rise shortly after its introduction nearly twenty years ago. It has been taken up not only by teachers of Classics, but by teachers of other subjects (modern languages or English). Ancient History is very popular in several states. There are, for example, over 3,000 students in Queensland studying Ancient History in each of Year 11 and Year

"Other states similarly have developed syllabuses which cater for the increased spread of interests and abilities of students . . ."

12—about one in every ten students. In South Australia teachers took the initiative in developing a new syllabus in Ancient Studies particularly for students who were not intending to go on to university; in addition, one in eight of those studying for matriculation takes Classical Studies. Other states similarly have developed syllabuses which cater for the increased spread of interests and abilities of students remaining at school until Year 12.

In New South Wales, Ancient History has had a niche since the early 1950s. In 1989 there were 8,450 (or one in six) students who took the subject for the Higher School Certificate (by way of comparison, 15,900 took Modern History). Ancient History is next in size of candidature after Modern History, Chemistry and Physics and ahead of Visual Arts, Home Science, Industrial Technology and Engineering Science. It has been suggested that the solid position of Ancient History in NSW schools goes back to A.H. McDonald who, as Professor of Ancient History at the University of Sydney, enthused a generation of teacher trainees, many with little or no qualifications in Latin or Greek, to teach Ancient as well as Modern History when they went out to schools. Many of their students in turn studied Ancient History at one of the five universities in NSW or the ACT that offer it, and those who became teachers are currently building up Ancient History numbers in their departments (whether History, English/History or Language departments). The current syllabus, in whose development I confess considerable involvement, has a strong emphasis on the development of historical skills. Students must apply these skills to at least two of the three areas: Near Eastern, Greek and Roman history. Within these areas no particular period is compulsory, though there is a tendency for teachers to focus students' attention on fifth-century Greece and Roman history from Sulla to the death of Nero—both compulsory periods under the previous syllabus. However, the lack of compulsion has encouraged teachers to select periods which were covered by very few schools previously. New themes based on archaeological evidence and new texts have also been taken up in many schools. The current syllabus provides an option, known as the 2 Unit General course, which is attractive for less able students; it offers a broad impression of various ancient societies along with a concentration on prominent personalities (such as Hatshepsut, Alexander and Agrippina the Younger) and their times. Even so, the syllabus is now due for revision. Teachers who are roped in to teach Ancient History with minimal background in the subject need more guidance in the syllabus documents. There is also a concern expressed by many teachers that skills using archaeological evidence and those using written evidence should be developed in all students, now that attention has been given for the duration of the present syllabus to archaeology as a source of evidence.

I have, of course, talked at some length about the situation I know best, but I should point out that there has been a parallel development in New Zealand. There the subject Classical Studies was introduced in 1980. Already in 1989 there were over 2,300 students taking it at matriculation ('Bursary' examination). The subject offers a choice of twenty Greek and Roman topics over the last two years of schooling, covering history, literature, drama, art, science, religion, and philosophy. A whole series of booklets has been written, largely by university staff in New Zealand, which schools can use as resources. The course has proved attractive to many students who have had no previous involvement with ancient world studies, and over a third of the teachers are not Classics graduates. The universities are now seeing the flow-on of students who have taken this new subject or seen their colleagues enjoy it. To take two examples: the number of 'effective full-time students'—the crucial figure for academic staffing decisions in that country as in this—doubled in the Classics Department of the University of Otago between 1985 and 1989; the student:staff ratio in the Classics Department of the University of Canterbury jumped from 13:1 in 1986 to 24:1 in 1990. In a context in which humanities departments, no matter how understaffed, repeatedly see their staff numbers reduced, additional posts in Classics have been made available in these two New Zealand universities.

". . . current bureaucratic and political thinking may prevent this demand being met."

There are signs that the strong demand for Classical Studies and Ancient History will remain, but current bureaucratic and political thinking may prevent this demand being met. The senior school curriculum is under review in several Australian states. Some educational administrators and government ministers have preconceived ideas as to which subjects students and their parents would prefer to have taught. Society and Culture, Legal Studies and (Contemporary) Australian Studies are some of the courses that are considered to be more immediately relevant to Australian school students. But there can be no doubt that the ancient world will continue to be attractive to students and their parents. Television series such as 'I Claudius' have been given a second and third run. Crowds have queued to see exhibitions over the decade from 'Pompeii AD 79' in 1979 to 'Ancient Macedonia' in 1989 and 'Civilization: Ancient Treasures from the British Museum' in 1990. Certainly university staff are keen to foster study of the ancient world in the schools. Most departments of Classics work closely with schools and provide students and teachers with lectures, in-service seminars, and guided tours of museum collections.

Many students take a Classical language or study Ancient History or Classical Literature in translation in order to improve their analytical skills or breadth of knowledge, or simply because of the intrinsic fascination of the ancient world. Motivations of this kind are particularly frequent among mature-age students at the universities. School leavers do seem to flock to Classical Studies at tertiary level in Victoria and New Zealand, or to Ancient History in (for example) New South Wales, partly because those were subjects taught in their schools. When the name is not that of a school subject, as with 'Classical Literature' in New South Wales, students who have lived a little come to it with greater understanding and seem to appreciate Homer, Sophocles or Virgil more.

But, of course, many students majoring in the Classical world are looking for a job at the end of their degree. In the United Kingdom, a survey of 1,500 graduates with intensive study of Greek and Latin showed that they found employment particularly in the 'commerce' sector (careers in financial, computer-related or retail areas, but not including 'industry') (Council of University Classical Departments, *Bulletin* no. 16, 1987), though one senior manager did comment that he used his Classical training more when he attended, and eventually came to chair, large international discussions of major economic issues than when he was keeping hand-written ledgers of lending to small companies (*The Times*, 23 May 1990). In Australia, a recent survey indicated that 'Employers are realising that humanities graduates in general have powers of analysis, expression and articulation that those trained in narrow technical areas lack. Those who have studied the Classics also come with a broader perspective into different cultures, which many employers see as important, particularly if recruits are likely to become managers and move into other areas. In a word, they are "flexible".' (William West, *The Weekend Australian*, 1–2 April 1989). Submissions made on the Commonwealth Government's Green Paper on Higher Education by employer and industry representatives said that they valued the analytical skills and adaptability of humanities students (Michelle Gunn, *Australian*, 31 January 1990). Students who began their study of Greek at Sydney University in 1989, in an evaluation of the unit, stressed in addition to its specific content the self-organisation and self-discipline they had acquired, an increase in their

"... employers seem to value ... a breadth of view which comes from studying other cultures in a holistic manner."

ability to analyse and criticise, and a greater understanding of English structure and grammar (Suzanne MacAlister, *Australian*, 21 February 1990). The qualities that employers seem to value in graduates with Classical training are intellectual rigour, the ability to communicate clearly, analytical skills, the ability to handle complex information and, above all, a breadth of view which comes from studying other cultures in a holistic manner.

APPENDIX 1

Books on the ancient world published 1965–1990

In addition to journal articles, reviews and other publications, the following books have been published by scholars while working in Australia during the period 1965–1990.

To avoid repetition, co-authored books have been listed only under the author named first on the title page; co-authors' names are given under that entry.

Art and Archaeology

D.S. Barrett, *Greek and Roman Coins in the University of Queensland*, Brisbane 1974, 2nd ed. 1982

J.M. Birmingham, *The Cypriot Bronze Age* (ed.), Sydney 1973

Alexander Cambitoglou, *The Brygos Painter*, Sydney 1968

——*Zagora 1: Excavations of a Geometric Settlement on the Island of Andros, Greece* (co-authors J.J. Coulton, J. Birmingham, J.R. Green), Sydney 1971

——*Studies in Honour of A.D. Trendall* (ed.), Sydney 1979

——*Archaeological Museum of Andros: Guide to the Finds from the Excavations of the Geometric Town at Zagora* (co-authors S. Peirce, O. Segal, J. Papadopoulos), Athens 1981

——*Le peintre de Darius et son milieu* (co-authors C. Aellen, J. Chamay), Genève 1986

——*Zagora 2: Excavations of a Geometric Settlement on the Island of Andros, Greece* (co-authors J.J. Coulton, A. Birchall, J.R. Green), Athens 1988

P.J. Connor, *Roman Art in the National Gallery of Victoria*, Melbourne 1978

A. Cremin, *The Enduring Past: Archaeology of the Ancient World for Australians* (ed.), Sydney 1987

J.L. Crowley, *The Aegean and the East: An Investigation into the Transference of Artistic Motifs between the Aegean, Egypt and the Near East in the Bronze Age*, Jonsered 1989

Jean-Paul Descoeudres, *Die vorklassische Keramik aus dem Gebiet des Westtors: Eretria, Ausgrabungen und Forschungen 5*, Bern 1976; *Eretria, Ausgrabungen und Forschungen 6* (co-authors C. Dunant, I.R. Metzger, C. Berard), Bern 1978

——*Corpus Vasorum Antiquorum, Basel I*, Bern 1981

——*Greek Colonists and Native Populations: Proceedings of the First Australian Congress of Classical Archaeology held in Honour of Emeritus Professor A.D. Trendall* (ed.), Oxford 1990

——*Ceramic and Iconographic Studies in Honour of Alexander Cambitoglou* (ed.), Sydney 1990

David Frankel, *Middle Cypriot White Painted Pottery: An Analytical Study of the Decoration*, Gothenburg 1974

——*Corpus of Cypriote Antiquities, 7: Early and Middle Bronze Age Material in the Ashmolean Museum, Oxford*, Gothenburg 1983

J.R. Green, *Gnathia Pottery in the Akademisches Kunstmuseum, Bonn,* Mainz 1976

——Revised and enlarged edition of T.B.L. Webster, *Monuments Illustrating Old and Middle Comedy,* London 1978
——*Corpus Vasorum Antiquorum, New Zealand I,* Oxford 1979
——*Antiquities: A Description of the Classics Department Museum in the Australian National University, Canberra* (with Beryl Rawson), Canberra 1981
——*Corpus Vasorum Antiquorum, The University Museum, Philadelphia I* (USA 22), Philadelphia 1986
R.G. Hood, *Greek Vases in the University of Tasmania*, 3rd ed. Hobart 1982
C.A. Hope, *Egyptian Pottery*, Aylesbury 1987
N. Kanawati, *The Rock Tombs of El Hawawish: The Cemetery of Akhmim,* vols. I–IX, Sydney 1980–89
——*Excavations at Saqqara: North-West of Teti's Pyramid,* vols. I–II, Sydney 1984–88
——*The Tomb and its Significance in Ancient Egypt*, Cairo 1987
——*A Mountain Speaks: The First Australian Expedition in Egypt,* Sydney 1988
——*Quseir El Amarna: The Tombs of Pepy-Ankh and Khewen-Wekh,* Sydney 1989
M.G. Kanowski, *The Antiquities Collection, Department of Classics and Ancient History*, Brisbane 1978
——*Containers of Classical Greece,* Brisbane 1984
——*Old Bones: Unlocking Archaeological Secrets*, Melbourne 1987
R.A. Kearsley, *The Pendent Semi-Circle Skyphos*, London 1989
Ian McPhee, *Greek Red-figured Fish-plates* (co-author A.D. Trendall), Basel 1987, with Addenda in *Antike Kunst* 33 (1990)
——*The Extramural Sanctuary of Demeter and Persephone at Cyrene* (co-author Donald White), Philadelphia 1990
J.R. Melville-Jones, *A Dictionary of Ancient Greek Coins*, London 1986
——*A Dictionary of Ancient Roman Coins*, London 1990
B.G. Ockinga, *Two Ramesside Tombs at El Mashayikh*, Sydney 1988
E.G. Pemberton, *Corinth, Volume XVIII, Part I: The Sanctuary of Demeter and Kore, The Greek Pottery*, Princeton 1989
Ronald T. Ridley, *The Unification of Egypt: As Seen Through a Study of the Major Knife-handles, Palettes and Maceheads*, Deception Bay 1973
F.B. Sear, *Roman Wall and Vault Mosaics*, Heidelberg 1977
——*Roman Architecture*, London and Ithaca 1982, 2nd rev. ed. 1989
——*The Museum of Classical Archaeology*, Adelaide 1988
A.D. Trendall, *South Italian Vase Painting*, London 1966, 2nd ed. 1976
——*Phlyax Vases*, 2nd ed. London 1967
——*The Red-figured Vases of Lucania, Campania and Sicily*, 2 vols., Oxford 1967, with Supplements London 1970, 1973, 1983
——*Greek Vases in the Logie Collection*, Christchurch 1971
——*Early South Italian Vases*, Mainz 1974
——*Vasi Antichi Dipinti del Vaticano: La Collezione Astarita III. Vasi Italiote ed Etruschi a Figure Rosse,* Vatican 1976
——*Greek Vases in the National Gallery of Victoria*, Melbourne 1978
——*Twenty Years of Progress in Classical Archaeology*, Sydney 1979
——*The Red-figured Vases of Paestum*, Rome 1987
——*The Red-figured Vases of South Italy and Sicily*, London 1989
In collaboration:
with T.B.L. Webster: *Illustrations of Greek Drama*, London 1971
with Margo Schmidt and Alexander Cambitoglou: *Eine Gruppe Apulischer Grabvasen in Basel*, Basel 1976

with Alexander Cambitoglou: *The Red-figured Vases of Apulia,* Oxford, vol. I, 1978; vol. II, 1982, with Supplement London 1983
with Marit R. Jentoft-Nilsen: *Corpus Vasorum Antiquorum*, USA 26, Paris 1990
K.H. Waters, *Greek Coins in the University of Tasmania*, Hobart 1981
——*Roman Coins in the University of Tasmania*, Hobart 1981–82

Classical Heritage

M.N. Austin, *An Ignorant Man Thinking*, Perth 1966
Graeme Clarke, *Rediscovering Hellenism: The Hellenic Inheritance and the English Imagination* (ed.), Cambridge 1989
——*Reading the Past in Late Antiquity* (ed. with B.Croke, R. Mortley and A. Emmett-Nobbs), Canberra 1989
B.F. Croke, *History and Historians in Late Antiquity* (co-editor A.M. Emmett), Sydney 1983
B.F. Harris, *Auckland Classical Essays Presented to E.M. Blaiklock* (ed. and contributor), Auckland 1970
Richard St Clair Johnson, *The Marriage of Mercury and Philology by Martianus Capella* (translated and edited with W.H. Stahl, E.L. Burge), New York, vol. I, 1971; vol. II, 1977
M.N. Kelly, *For Service to Classical Studies: Essays in Honour of Francis Letters* (ed.), Melbourne 1966
Ann Moffatt, *Maistor: Classical, Byzantine and Renaissance Studies for Robert Browning* (ed. and contributor), Canberra 1984
——Paul Lemerle. *Byzantine Humanism, The First Phase: Notes and Remarks on Education and Culture in Byzantium from its Origins to the 10th Century,* trans. with Helen Lindsay, Canberra 1986
Raoul Mortley, *Désir et différence dans la tradition platonicienne,* Paris 1988
M.E. Mullett, *Byzantium and the Classical Tradition* (co-editor R.D. Scott), Birmingham 1981
J.A. Willis, *Martianus Capella, De nuptiis Philologiae et Mercurii* (ed.), Leipzig 1983

Early Christianity and Related Studies

F.I. Andersen, *Job: An Introduction and Commentary*, Leicester 1976
——*A Linguistic Concordance of Ruth and Jonah: Hebrew Vocabulary and Idiom.* Wooster 1976
——*Eight Minor Prophets: A Linguistic Concordance*, Wooster 1976
——*A Linguistic Concordance of Jeremiah: Hebrew Vocabulary and Idiom*, Wooster 1978
——*A Linguistic Concordance of Jeremiah: Common Nouns and Verbs*, Wooster 1978
——*Hosea: A New Translation with Introduction and Commentary,* New York 1980
——*Amos: A New Translation with Introduction and Commentary* (co-author D.N. Freedman), New York 1989
R.J. Banks, *Jesus and the Law in the Synoptic Tradition*, Cambridge 1975
——*Paul's Idea of Community: The Earliest House-Churches in their Historical Setting,* Sydney 1979
P.W. Barnett, *Is the New Testament History?* Sydney 1986
——*The Message of II Corinthians: Power in Weakness*, Leicester 1988
——*Bethlehem to Patmos: The New Testament Story*, Sydney 1989
——*Apocalypse Now and Then: Reading Revelation Today*, Sydney 1989
——*The Two Faces of Jesus*, Sydney 1990

Graeme Clarke, *The Octavius of Marcus Minucius Felix*, New York 1974
——*The Letters of St Cyprian*, vols. 1–4, New York 1984–89
B.F. Croke, *Religious Conflict in Fourth-century Rome: A Documentary Study* (co-author J. Harrier), Sydney 1982
G.H.R. Horsley, *New Documents Illustrating Early Christianity: A Review of the Greek Inscriptions and Papyri Published*, vols. 1–4, Sydney 1981–87
——*New Documents Illustrating Early Christianity*, vol.5, *Linguistic Essays*, Sydney 1989
E.A. Judge, *The Conversion of Rome: Ancient Sources of Modern Social Tensions*, Sydney 1980
——*Rank and Status in the World of the Caesars and St Paul*, Christchurch 1982
J.A.L. Lee, *A Lexical Study of the Septuagint Version of the Pentateuch*, Chico 1983
R.J. Maddox, *Witnesses to the End of the Earth: The Pattern of Mission in the Book of Acts*, Sydney 1980.
P.J. Marshall, *Enmity at Corinth: Social Conventions in Paul's Relations with the Corinthians*, Tübingen 1987
Raoul Mortley, *Connaissance religieuse et herméneutique chez Clément d'Alexandrie*, Leiden 1973
——*From Word to Silence:* vol. I, *The Rise and Fall of Logos;* vol. II, *The Way of Negation, Christian and Greek*, Bonn 1986
B.G. Ockinga, *Die Gottebenbildlichkeit im Alten Ägypten und im Alten Testament*, Wiesbaden 1984

Greek History

R.A. Bauman, *Political Trials in Ancient Greece*, London 1990
A.B. Bosworth, *A Historical Commentary on Arrian's History of Alexander*, vol. I, Oxford 1980
——*From Arrian to Alexander: Studies in Historical Interpretation*, Oxford 1988
——*Conquest and Empire: The Reign of Alexander the Great*, Cambridge 1988
V.G. Callender, *The Minoans*, Sydney 1987
R. Develin, *Athenian Officials 684–321 B.C.*, Cambridge 1989
J.R. Ellis, *The Spectre of Philip: A Study in Historical Evidence* (co-author R.D. Milns), Sydney 1970, repr. 1977
——*Philip II and Macedonian Imperialism*, London 1976
L. Fitzhardinge, *The Spartans*, London 1980
A. French, *The Athenian Half-Century*, Sydney 1971
——*Sixth Century Athens: The Sources*, Sydney 1987
J.R. Green, *Ancient Athens*, Wellington 1971
Alan S. Henry, *Supplementum Epigraphicum Graecum*, vol. XXV (ed. A.G. Woodhead, with J. Bousquet, A.S. Henry, T.B. Mitford), Leiden 1971
——*The Prescripts of Athenian Decrees, Mnemosyne Supplement* vol. 49, Leiden 1977
——*Honours and Privileges in Athenian Decrees: The Principal Formulae of Athenian Honorary Decrees, Subsidia Epigraphica*, vol. X, Hildesheim 1983
G.H.R. Horsley, *Hellenika: Essays on Greek History and Politics* (ed. and contributor), Sydney 1982
Roger Just, *Women in Athenian Law and Life*, London and New York 1989
M.N. Kelly, *View from Olympus*, 2nd ed. Melbourne 1986
D.W. Knight, *Some Studies in Athenian Politics in the Fifth Century B.C.*, Wiesbaden 1970
Arthur S. McDevitt, *Inscriptions from Thessaly: An Analytical Handlist and Bibliography*, Hildesheim and New York 1970

R.D. Milns, *Alexander the Great*, London 1968
Michael J. Osborne, *Lexicon of Greek Personal Names*, vol. II, *Athens*, Oxford 1990
R.K. Sinclair, *Democracy and Participation in Athens*, Cambridge 1988, repr. 1989
G.R. Stanton, *Athenian Politics c.800–c.500 B.C.*, London and New York 1990
K.H. Waters, *Herodotus on Tyrants and Despots*, Wiesbaden 1971
——*Herodotos the Historian*, London 1985

Greek Language and Literature

Michael Apthorp, *The Manuscript Evidence for Interpolation in Homer*, Heidelberg 1980
C. De Heer, *Makar, Eudaimon, Olbios, Eutyches: A Study of the Semantic Field Denoting Happiness in Ancient Greek to the End of the 5th Century B.C.*, Amsterdam 1969
Michael Ewans, *Wagner and Aeschylus: The 'Ring' and 'Oresteia'*, London 1982
G.H. Gellie, *Sophocles: A Reading*, Melbourne 1972
Alan S. Henry, *Basic Greek Course*, Clayton 1976
——*Teach Yourself Ancient Greek* (co-author G.G. Betts), Sevenoaks 1989
Alan W. James, *Studies in the Language of Oppian of Cilicia*, Amsterdam 1970
——*Index in Halieutica Oppiani Cilicis et in Cynegetica Poetae Apameensis*, Hildesheim and New York 1970
Kevin Lee, *Euripides: Troades*, ed. with Introduction and Commentary, London 1976
——*Index of Passages cited in W. Breitenbach, Untersuchungen zur Sprache der euripideischen Lyrik*, Amsterdam 1979
K.L. McKay, *Greek Grammar for Students: A Concise Grammar of Classical Attic with Special Reference to Aspect in the Verb*, Canberra 1974, repr. 1977
——*Manthano: An Introductory Course in Classical Greek for University Students*, Canberra 1975, repr. 1982
George P. Shipp, *Studies in the Language of Homer*, 2nd ed. Cambridge 1972
——ΝΟΜΟΣ "Law", Sydney 1978
——*Modern Greek Evidence for the Ancient Greek Vocabulary*, Sydney 1979
R.G. Ussher, *Sophocles: Philoctetes*, Warminster 1990

Greek and Roman Philosophy

H.A.K. Hunt, *A Physical Interpretation of the Universe: The Doctrines of Zeno the Stoic*, Melbourne 1976
D.G. Londey, *The Logic of Apuleius* (co-author C.J. Johanson), Leiden 1987
Raoul Mortley, *The Problem of Knowledge in Late Antiquity*, Berkeley 1978
——*Ancient Mysticism: Greek and Christian Mysticism, and some Comparisons with Buddhism*, Sydney 1980
——*Womanhood: The Feminine in Ancient Hellenism, Gnosticism, Christianity and Islam*, Sydney 1981
——*The Via Negativa* (co-editor D.W. Dockrill), Auckland 1982
H.A.S. Tarrant, *Scepticism or Platonism?* Cambridge 1985

Latin Language and Literature

R.J. Baker, *Propertius I, Translated with Introduction, Literary Commentary and Latin Text*, Armidale 1990
J.H. Bishop, *The Cost of Power: A Study of the Aeneid of Virgil*, Armidale 1988
A.J. Boyle, *Ancient Pastoral* (ed.), Melbourne 1975
——*The Eclogues of Virgil*, Melbourne 1976
——*Virgil's Ascraean Song* (ed.), Melbourne 1983

——*Seneca Tragicus* (ed.), Melbourne 1983
——*The Chaonian Dove: Studies in the Eclogues, Georgics and Aeneid of Virgil,* Leiden 1986
——*Seneca's Phaedra,* Liverpool 1987
——*The Imperial Muse: To Juvenal Through Ovid* (ed.), Melbourne 1988
P.J. Connor, *Horace's Lyric Poetry: The Force of Humour,* Melbourne 1987
C.G. Cooper, *Journey to Hesperia: Scenes from the First Six Books of Vergil's Aeneid,* 2nd ed. London 1965
H.D. Jocelyn, *The Tragedies of Ennius,* Cambridge 1969
P. McGushin, *C. Sallustius Crispus, Bellum Catilinae: A Commentary,* Leiden 1977
——*Sallust, Bellum Catilinae* (ed.), Bristol 1980
——*The Transmission of the Punica of Silius Italicus,* Amsterdam 1985
——*Sallust: The Conspiracy of Catiline: A Companion to the Penguin Translation*, Bristol 1987
C.J. Mackie, *The Characterisation of Aeneas,* Edinburgh 1988
J.R.C. Martyn, *Friedländer's Essays on Juvenal* (ed.), Amsterdam 1969
——*Cicero and Virgil: Studies in Honour of Harold Hunt* (ed.), Amsterdam 1972
——*D. Iuni Iuvenalis Saturae* (ed.), Amsterdam 1989
F. Muecke, *A Companion to the Menaechmi of Plautus*, Bristol 1987
C.E.V. Nixon, *Pacatus: Panegyric to the Emperor Theodosius* (ed.), Liverpool 1983
H.D. Rankin, *Petronius the Artist: Essays on the Satyricon and its Author*, The Hague 1971
A.C. Romano, *Irony in Juvenal*, Hildesheim 1979
A. Treloar, *Horace the Minstrel* (co-author N.A. Bonavia-Hunt), Kineton 1969
Lindsay Watson, *Arae: The Curse Poetry of Antiquity*, Leeds 1990
J.A. Willis, *Macrobii Saturnalia* (ed.), 2 vols., 2nd ed. Leipzig 1970
——*Latin Textual Criticism*, Illinois 1972

Roman History

R.A. Bauman, *The Crimen Maiestatis in the Roman Republic and Augustan Principate,* Johannesburg 1967
——*Impietas in Principem*, Munich 1974
——*Lawyers in Roman Republican Politics,* Munich 1983
——*Lawyers in Roman Transitional Politics*, Munich 1985
——*Lawyers and Politics in the Early Roman Empire*, Munich 1989
J. Bellemore, *Nicolaus of Damascus, Life of Augustus* (ed.), Bristol 1984
R. Develin, *Patterns in Office-Holding: 366–49 B.C.,* Brussels 1979
——*The Practice of Politics at Rome 366–167 B.C.,* Brussels 1979
Suzanne Dixon, *The Roman Mother*, London 1988
A.J. Dunston, *Essays on Roman Culture: The Todd Memorial Lectures* (ed.), Toronto and Sarasota 1976
B.W. Jones, *Domitian and the Senatorial Order: A Prosopographical Study of Domitian's Relationship with the Senate, A.D. 81–96*, Philadelphia 1979
——*The Use of Documentary Evidence in the Study of Roman Imperial History* (co-author R.D. Milns), Sydney 1984
——*The Emperor Titus*, London 1984
E.J. Jory, *Inscriptiones Vrbis Romae Latinae, consilio et auctoritate Academiae Scientiarum Reipublicae Democraticae Germanicae editum, Voluminis sexti pars septima fasciculi I–VI,* Berlin 1974–5, *fasc. VII*, Berlin 1989
E.A. Judge, *On Judging the Merits of Augustus*, Berkeley 1985

M.N. Kelly, *View from the Forum,* Melbourne 1969, 2nd ed. 1989
Bruce A. Marshall, *Crassus: A Political Biography,* Amsterdam 1976
——*A Historical Commentary on Asconius*, Columbia 1985
J. Mottershead, *Suetonius: Claudius* (ed.), Bristol 1986
Beryl Rawson, *The Politics of Friendship: Pompey and Cicero,* Sydney 1978, repr. 1981
——*The Family in Ancient Rome: New Perspectives* (ed. and contributor), London and Ithaca 1986
——*Marriage, Divorce and Children in Ancient Rome* (ed. and contributor), Oxford 1990
Ronald T. Ridley, *New History: Zosimus* (trans. with commentary), Sydney 1982
——*The History of Rome,* Rome 1987
P.R.C. Weaver, *Familia Caesaris*, Cambridge 1972

Other

D.S. Barrett, *Previews and Reruns: Readings Illustrating a Comparative Approach to Ancient History*, Brisbane 1976, 2nd rev. ed. 1977
——*Threshold of Time* (co-authors T.R. Bryce, M.G. Kanowski), Sydney 1977
——*A Map History of the Ancient World* (co-authors T.R. Bryce, M.G. Kanowski), Melbourne 1987
T.R. Bryce, *Pathways to the Past* (co-authors R. Joyce *et al.*), Sydney 1975
——*The Major Historical Texts of Early Hittite History,* Brisbane 1983
——*Historical and Social Documents of the Hittite World,* Brisbane 1983
——*The Lycians, A Study of Lycian History and Civilisation to the Conquest of Alexander the Great,* vol. I, *The Lycians in Literary and Epigraphic Sources*, Copenhagen 1986
C.B. Forbes, *Documents of the Egyptian Empire, 1550–1350 B.C.,* Melbourne 1981
——*Documents of the Assyrian Empire, 1115–612 B.C.*, Melbourne 1987
J.R. Green, *The Wonders of the Ancient World,* Sydney 1977
E.M. Jeffreys, *The Chronicle of John Malalas: A Translation* (co-authors M.J. Jeffreys, R.D. Scott, with B. Croke, J. Ferber, S. Franklin, A. James, D. Kelly, A. Moffatt, A. Nixon), Melbourne 1986
——*Studies in John Malalas* (co-editors B. Croke, R.D. Scott), Sydney 1990
B.W. Jones, *Register of Oxyrhynchites, 30 B.C.–A.D. 96* (co-author J. Whitehorne), Chico 1983
N. Kanawati, *The Egyptian Administration in the Old Kingdom: Evidence on its Economic Decline,* Warminster 1977
——*Governmental Reforms in Old Kingdom Egypt*, Warminster 1980
Bruce A. Marshall, *Vindex Humanitatis: Essays in Honour of John Huntly Bishop* (ed.), Armidale 1980
R.D. Milns, *Foreign Languages in Queensland* (ed.), Brisbane 1974
S.R. Pickering, *Papyrus Editions,* Sydney 1984
J.E.G. Whitehorne, *Strategi and Royal Scribes of Roman Egypt: Chronological List and Index* (co-author G. Bastianini), Florence 1987
Ian Worthington, *Acta of the University of New England International Seminar on Greek and Latin Epigraphy* (ed.), Bonn 1990

(Compiled by Beryl Rawson and Edyth Binkowski with ASCS university representatives, whose assistance is gratefully acknowledged.)

APPENDIX 2

Thematic conferences and seminars

In addition to the regular conferences held by the Australian Society for Classical Studies, at which papers are given on a wide range of topics, there have been more specialised thematic conferences and seminars since 1969. These became more frequent in the late 1970s and have occurred every year since 1981—usually more than one per year. Some seminars have been built around an overseas visitor at one institution. More broadly based seminars have had themes in the following areas:

Greek and Roman history (Universities of Melbourne 1969, 1985, 1988, Tasmania 1976, 1984, Monash 1977, Sydney 1979, 1985, Queensland 1984, 1987, New England 1988, Humanities Research Centre at the Australian National University 1981, 1985, 1988)
historiography of Greece and Rome, late antiquity and the classical heritage (Macquarie 1981, HRC at the ANU 1981, 1985, 1988)
Byzantine studies (HRC at the ANU 1978, 1985)
art and archaeology (Sydney 1973, 1985, HRC and the Australian National Gallery 1990, Monash and the Museum of Victoria 1990)
Greek philosophy (Sydney 1978, 1982, 1985, 1986, 1990, Newcastle 1984)
Greek and Roman literature and drama (Sydney 1982, 1983, Tasmania 1987, 1988, Bendigo CAE 1989, Queensland 1989, New England 1990)
Greek and Latin epigraphy (Tasmania 1984, New England 1989)
religions (Newcastle 1990).

APPENDIX 3

Office-bearers of the Australian Society for Classical Studies

President

A.D. Trendall (1966–7)	H.A.K. Hunt (1967–9)	A.J. Dunston (1969–70)
H.D. Rankin (1970–1)	K.L. McKay (1971–3)	J.R. Trevaskis (1973–4)
K.H. Waters (1974–5)	J.H. Bishop (1975–6)	G.W. Clarke (1976–8)
W. Ritchie (1978–80)	G.H. Gellie (1980–1)	P.R.C. Weaver (1981–3)
K.J. McKay (1983–5)	A. French (1985–6)	T.R. Bryce (1986–8)
B.M. Rawson (1988–9)	R.K. Sinclair (1989–)	

Vice-President

J.H. Bishop (1966–70)	G.W. Clarke (1970–1)	J.R. Trevaskis (1971–3)
K.L. McKay (1973–6)	J.H. Bishop (1976–8)	G.W. Clarke (1978–80)
W. Ritchie (1980–1)	G.H. Gellie (1981–3)	P.R.C. Weaver (1983–5)
K.J. McKay (1985–6)	A. French (1986–8)	D.H. Kelly (1988–9)
B.M. Rawson (1989–)		

Secretary

K.L. McKay (1966–70)	A.S. Henry (1970–3)	J.R. Ellis (1973–7)
B.A. Marshall (1977–87)	R.A. Pitcher (1987–)	

Treasurer

R.K. Sinclair (1966–74) A.W. James (1974–)

Editors

E.A. Judge, W. Ritchie (1966–73)	E.A. Judge, K.J. McKay (1973–4)
K.J. McKay, P.R.C. Weaver (1974–83)	K.J. McKay, R. Mortley (1983–5)
R. Mortley, G.R. Stanton (1985–90)	G.R. Stanton, R.J. Baker (1990–)